Good Goodbyes

Raves about **Good Goodbyes**

"Joan Grey accomplishes so much in this book, that my medical training and family practice over 30 years never did for me. Most people expect healthcare professionals to know how to prepare their patients and families for the inevitable day when we pass. Not at all.

"Joan uses wit, acronyms, alliteration, and a wealth of references to help all of us prepare for the inevitable – our death. While not a topic most embrace – she raises the case to prepare for our departure if not for us – for those we love and leave behind.

"Pages of practical actionable advice that we all could take to help prepare ourselves, family, and friends for what no one is likely to escape. Stories illustrate the positive impact we can make if we just stop and learn more about what we can do now. As a family physician trained over 30 years ago – there was more information and advice in this book than I have seen before. Physicians, nurses, and most healthcare professionals DO NOT know how or train for helping others in death. And yet perhaps the real responsibility is the individual.

"*Good Goodbyes* is well organized and referenced yet written with illustrative stories and wit to inspire us to accept this ultimate responsibility ourselves."

- Bill Lynagh, MD

"*Good Goodbyes* is profound, inspirational, and motivational. Death characterized as a threshold to eternity is serene and comforting.

Choosing how we spend our time and formulating a love letter that lasts resonate with me. We all have stories to tell. I want to make sure mine are told and that loved ones have cherished memories to reflect on. I want to spend time with those who care about me, use simple words of love, and write letters to my children and grandchildren for significant future milestones in their lives – my way of being present. Lastly, I plan to set aside objects that each might want as a tangible reminder of me."

- Amy Murrell, West Point 1980 classmate

"Planning ahead for our good goodbyes is so easy to put off and leave on the back burner. *Good Goodbyes* is so well thought out and filled with good ideas."

- Cathy Sterling: Nana, Weaver, Army spouse, Loving Friend

"I think this is an extremely valuable book, especially in the detailed and sensible recommendations it makes."

- Kevin Madigan, Winn Professor of Ecclesiastical History, Harvard Divinity School

"Joan is offering a book I would certainly want to read in full. She makes an interesting comparison with a wildly successful guide to the other end of life, *What to Expect When You're Expecting*, which was published 36 years ago by Workman Publishing, which now owns Algonquin Books, the company I helped found."

- Shannon Purves, former editor, Algonquin Books

Good Goodbyes

A Mortal's Guide to Life

Joan S. Grey

Opus One Studios
8641 Elm Street, Suite 1154
McLean, VA 22101
www.opusonestudios.com

ISBN: 978-1-73649-663-3

Cover and Interior Design by Brent Spears

Behold! I make all things new.[1]

WHAT THE CATERPILLAR CALLS THE END,
THE REST OF THE WORLD CALLS A
BUTTERFLY.
LAO TZU

DEDICATION

Embrace the threshold.
Where we began, so we'll end.[2]

∞

ALL PROFITS TO CHARITY

Buying *Good Goodbyes* will not only help set the stage
for your good goodbye but will benefit West Point Women.
The West Point Women's Conference Endowment is designated
as the "worthy cause," which will receive 100% of the publisher's
and author's profits generated by sales of this book.

https://www.westpointaog.org/waystogive

CONTENTS

FOREWORD

Nobody wants to talk about dying. But *Good Goodbyes* liberates us to acknowledge that death is part of life—we may call it "unfortunate" but the ending is the price we pay for living. We need *Good Goodbyes* to help us prepare for the inevitable. As Mel Brooks says, "Live life! No one gets out alive."

Read this book through—enjoy the imagery, the well-chosen words, the research, and the humor. Then use this loving, gentle call to action as your workbook or guide – write in it and 'dog-ear' the pages.

Learn, Reflect, Act—be aware and then prepare—what is more important than working on your legacy and your love letter to the cherished people in your life? You might discover that life is stronger than death.

Joan Grey tackles a difficult subject with honesty and humor and gently guides us to prepare a legacy of love.

Jane F. Collen,
Intellectual Property Lawyer, author of historical fiction series
The Journey of Cornelia Rose, and the children's book series
The Enjella Adventure Series

PREFACE:

LIFE HAPPENS[3]

...

In my 20s, I was an Army paratrooper with what seemed like a predictable path ahead. Those assumptions failed during a nighttime tactical parachute mission. In the afternoon before parachuting, I had gone for a run. That night I collided in mid-air with another parachutist. The resulting hard landing and paralyzing injuries launched me into surgeries, treatments, and rehabilitation. My career in the Army was over, and my health wasn't in great shape either. Doctors weren't sure I'd walk again. An initial surgery fixed my spine for wheeling, not walking. It turns out that the paralysis was incomplete. I eventually learned to walk, but that run was seared in memory as my last run—ever.

I wanted my old life back. It took a long time, but ultimately I recognized the futility of knocking on the proverbial closed door. I hadn't died, but parts of my life were gone and there was no going back. I needed to come to terms with where I was and who I could become. Not resurrection, but transformation.

With the Army over, I used my experiences and became a hospital chaplain. Having paid the tuition, I could share my lessons by serving patients and families in their time of need. I encountered many things as a chaplain, but the biggest insight: most people have a delusional sense of safety. They don't think the reality of mortality applies to them. Few I ministered to were prepared for illness, injury, or dying.

That magical thinking applied to me too. While studying for a master's degree in religion, I had three close calls. In sequential years, I was trapped on a train during a fatal fire, barely avoided a tree falling in front of my car on the highway, and got hit by a bus while biking. It took the bus accident to connect the dots and reveal life's cardinal rule: you just never know. Any of those incidents could have been an exit instead of a detour.

On the Metro train awaiting rescue, I had 45 minutes lying on a dirty carpet to wonder: What if this is it? If I don't make it out alive, how much of a mess am I leaving behind?

That question continues to haunt and motivate. I wrote my thesis —*Awakening to Mortality: End-of-life as Rite of Passage and Pathway to Transformation*—as an initial response. With its approval, I completed degree requirements and graduated from Harvard in 2019.

The next step is this book: *Good Goodbyes: A Mortal's Guide to Life*. While conducting thesis research, I identified a gap. If you decide to get your affairs in order, what's the process? Who's the guide? Where are the books? Who conducts pre-mortem Lamaze classes? End-of-life is professionalized and atomized: doctors try to fix body parts; attorneys draft legal documents; ministers extol a heavenly reward. Is that what it's all about? You may argue: "But wait, doctors will be there at the end." Yes, but trying to keep you alive. *Dead* is not a good patient outcome. Treatments are billable. Death equals failure.

Except that our outcome is a certainty—we don't get out alive. And, because we revere beginnings and revile endings, we close our eyes to what's ahead. Which means when we or someone we love reaches that predictable stage, the reality can overwhelm. We're not the first to walk the end-of-life path, but denial, delusion, and delay force us to bushwhack a trail and learn as we go. And then we wonder: "Why didn't someone tell me? Why didn't I know this ahead of time?" We will all face situations when we wish we could hit *stop* and *rewind*. Sharing my hard-won insights won't spare you trauma, but it could make you just a bit better prepared.

During my research and writing, I was reminded of touring the Spinal Cord Injury Center as a new patient. I commented on the facility's accessible design for those "*confined* to wheelchairs." The staff member set me straight. With what seemed like a rehearsed rebuke: "A wheelchair *liberates*. *Confined* is when someone who needs a chair doesn't have one." That exchange made me see mobility and assistive devices in a new light. I hope *Good Goodbyes* might reframe death and inspire you to think differently about mortality. You may not be inclined to befriend the end, but maybe *Good Goodbyes* will change your perspective. Death may be a hard boundary, but we imprison ourselves with self-inflicted fear and failure to face reality. Is it possible for the end to be a liberating force rather than a limiting constraint?

Life can change in an instant. Crashing into the ground shattered body parts, smashed the illusion of invulnerability, and opened my eyes. Chaplaincy, the Metro, tree, bus, and whatever comes next remind:

there will come a time, when time is up. And a grace period isn't promised to get our act together. A good goodbye doesn't happen by chance.

We don't know when a run or a kiss will be the last, so ask yourself:

- Have I said what needs to be said and done what needs to be done?
- Have I taken steps that will make it easier for those left behind?
- Have I considered what will bring me a sense of peace and completion?

You don't know how much time you have, but you do have a choice: you can…

Go it alone. If so, blessings on the journey.

Or learn from my mistakes, experiences, and research.

And keep reading *Good Goodbyes*.

Just don't go without saying goodbye.

A light in the tunnel
Metro smoke, January 2015

INTRODUCTION

There's no going back.
The beginning can't be changed.
Start now. Change the end.[4]

A woman appears at the emergency room, with a man holding her arm. Her belly's distended and she winces in pain. In-between contractions, she beams; she's been waiting for this day. Her baby is about to be born. The emergency department personnel smile as they watch the couple head to obstetrics. Since her pregnancy was confirmed months ago, a detailed birthing plan has been a work-in-progress. The couple have already toured the posh birthing suite, attended childbirth classes, and selected a gourmet meal for a post-delivery celebration. They know where to go, what to do, and are ready to welcome their new family member. Life is good.

An elderly man staggers into the emergency department, gasping and grabbing his chest. Before he can be wheeled to the trauma bay, he loses consciousness and slumps down. Who is he? How old is he? Is he on medications? Does he have pre-existing conditions? Who's his next of kin? The man seems to have arrived alone and now he can't talk. A nurse finds a driver's license in the patient's wallet, so they know name, age, and address. That's a start, but critical information is missing. The care team does a physical exam and orders labs, trying to get a preliminary diagnosis as the treatment golden hour ticks down. A blank slate and educated guesses may not be enough when minutes count.

Birth and death are flip sides of the coin of life. But how differently we treat them. We revere the beginning. Within several generations, childbirth has changed from a doctor-centered, mother-sedated, father-excluded medical event to expecting a holistic, momentous experience, with the pregnant woman well-prepared, and to a certain extent calling the shots, for what lies ahead.

And what about the ending? Death is often a technology-assisted, patient-sedated, family-excluded medical event. Not a profound metamorphosis but an isolating, unconscious, physical failure. Which COVID-19 has only made worse… Why?

We don't like death.

We don't like to think about it.

We don't like to talk about it.

We pretend the day will never come.

We thought we'd have more time.

This isn't what I expected.

It's always too soon until it's too late. Eventually, our date with destiny arrives, a D-day that might range from the ultimate four-letter word *dead* to another devastating D-word variant—divorce, dementia, disease, disaster. We associate death with pain, something we're hard-wired to avoid. Avoiding makes it seem like we're protecting ourselves and those we love, but the very thing that we try to ignore eventually shows up. Mortality, like gravity, is a force of nature. We can fight it – temporarily. And our "never say die" approach means that we're blindsided, unprepared, and scrambling to deal with a predictable, and yet unpredictable, event. Our failing to be aware and prepared may make dying harder for us and for those we love.

Good Goodbyes: A Mortal's Guide to Life presents a holistic approach for a universal problem. It's a wake-up call, an organizing system, and inspiration for getting your affairs in order. We can't change death – our ultimate outcome – but it's possible for dying to be more of a transcendent passage rather than a medical crisis. Most people don't intend to leave a mess behind, but failing to anticipate and plan results in a chaotic conclusion. *Good Goodbyes* aims to inform, encourage, and empower you by providing indispensable information, practical advice, and reflective insights. A plan, a process, and a list can make your journey easier. Getting your end-of-life act together can be a love letter that lasts. The book's organizing framework – Aware, Prepare, Share and Care – corresponds to perspectives of head, hands, and heart, encompassed in whole: Spirit. Being Aware, being Prepared, and Sharing because you Care are a means to the end; love is the bottom line. Moving from good intentions to thoughtful actions can ease burdens and bring peace of mind.

Removing the blinders lets us approach the end of life as intentionally as we prepare for birth, and perhaps help make this entirely expected stage transformative rather than catastrophic. *Good Goodbyes'* holistic approach can ease fears of the unknown by providing a system, tools, and checklists. Being aware of the road ahead, considering preferences, preparing documents, and sharing information can take some of the mayhem out of mourning.

I am honored that you have chosen to explore life's final transition with me. As you read, use ideas that resonate; ignore what doesn't fit. Just don't go without saying goodbye.

ONE:

THE *OTHER* TALK

Responsible parents tell their children about how babies come into being. Having "The Talk" about the facts of life may feel awkward but is essential to protect our children. They need to know. When a woman gets pregnant, abundant resources explain the process she'll be going through. A first-time mother especially has many questions: What should I expect? What's normal? What do I need to watch out for? What should I be worried about? How can I relieve this symptom? Guidebooks and websites provide support, encouragement, and guidance every step of the way. We teach about reproduction and pregnancy, but we shouldn't stop there. Here's the thing: contraception can prevent birth, but there's no lasting prophylaxis against death. It's part of the human condition that no one escapes. The price of life is dying. Maybe the date will occur decades in the future, but the countdown timer starts at birth. Not everyone will face pregnancy. But dying – we're all in it together, no matter how much we deny or try to postpone the reality. It's not a secret, but you wouldn't know it by our attitudes and actions. Fear and squeamishness make death topic non grata—"that which must not be named" exacerbated by our "see no evil, hear no evil, speak no evil" rules of engagement. Yes. The idea of impermanence is scary and disorienting, but it's compounded by failing to talk about it and lacking resources for navigating the inevitability.

Good Goodbyes: A Mortal's Guide to Life includes the facts of life about the end of life. Even if you find the topic distressing, know that your preparation will make it easier for yourself and others. Dying well is about living well and may mean coming to terms with omissions and mistakes. It isn't about a high-tech respirator, designer hospital gown, or the most expensive ICU room. You'll get no bonus points for having a famous doctor, the longest scar, or most surgeries. Expecting a Goldilocks fairy-tale scenario – not too soon, not too late – can result in a nightmare. Ignoring the facts may feel like it eases the pain, but it may be setting a trap, hurting ourselves and the people we love.

We don't know when, where, or how. There are many things we can't control. But there are things we can change. Now more than ever, having lived through the COVID times, this information is vital. Take a chance. Take some time. Stay with me as we explore some of the things I've found out and figured out. I hope you'll use *Good Goodbyes* as a prompt to consider situations you might encounter as life is ending. But remember, the best time to think and act is when there's not a cloud in the sky.

Pain

We equate dying with pain. Hopefully, your doctors will control physical pain and ensure you're comfortable because bodily pain can overwhelm. When you're hurting physically, it's hard to think about much else. But, this pain is just the tip of the iceberg. There's also existential pain, the anguish associated with staring into the abyss. It's almost impossible to wrap our heads around not being, so this ache has no quick, overnight relief. And then there's emotional pain. No amount of preparation helps. No matter how ready we are, separation from loved ones will hurt. Sadness is the price we pay for love. We can't solve death, but shining light can make it less scary. To fix a problem, we must first face it. And finally, there's the pain of undone practicalities: pretending won't protect us; ignoring won't bring peace. We can spare others by preparing ahead of time for death's inevitable arrival, instead of compounding the pain. We can have our affairs organized rather than paying pain forward and leaving survivors with a mess to clean up.

Gain: Why the Information in *Good Goodbyes* is important

"Clear is kind. Unclear is unkind."[5]

Instead of viewing this work as estate planning—a phrase that evokes sterile, complicated legal documents—consider this as legacy or PEACE planning. Doing the work outlined in *Good Goodbyes* can ease fears by providing an idea of what to expect, making it easier for those we love. While death has no antidote, following the steps outlined in *Good Goodbyes* can lead to PEACE.

- **P**eace of mind
- **E**xpression of love
- **A**utonomy extender
- **C**haos control
- **E**ase burdens

The difference between an adventure and an ordeal is planning. If we consider the end of life as an open-book test, we realize that we can use whatever resource materials we want. We even know the questions ahead of time. The only tricky thing – the date. We don't know when we'll sit the exam. Don't go in empty-handed or cram at the last minute. Being unprepared sets you up for an ambush, with your family suffering collateral damage.

The end of life is a rite of passage. Like pregnancy, it requires practical, relational, and spiritual preparation. We will only get one chance to do dying right. Tedious work now can minimize grievous pain later. If you knew a few hours of effort could make a life-changing difference, would you do it? You can leave a legacy of love by relieving family members' burdens. Put yourself in your survivors' shoes and pay love forward. Having your house in order will provide a source of peace and comfort.

Audience

Not everyone will get pregnant, but everyone alive dies. It may be hard to convince a young adult of mortality, but most everyone on the north side of sixty recognizes that, barring a scientific miracle, they are over halfway to dead. And they have likely had the vicarious experience of someone else's dying. How did that go? Was it a good goodbye? If what you've seen is not what you want, there is an alternative. But it will require bravery. Are you up to it? A happier ending takes planning and preparation. Reading *Good Goodbyes* shows good intentions. The harder part is putting the steps into practice. We can make excuses: "I didn't know" or "I was scared." When the end comes, it requires courage. Can you be a hero? Not the jumping-on-a-grenade kind of bravery, but a willingness to face reality, knowing your family's happiness is at stake.

Questions To Consider:

- What does it mean to have "affairs in order"?
- Is a happy ending possible and if so, what does it take?
- What can I expect as end-of-life approaches?
- Won't a doctor be there to guide me and my family?

When I decided to organize our family's affairs, it seemed overwhelming, confusing, and off-putting. Each state with its proprietary forms added to the haphazard, fragmented, and convoluted process. But, it needed to get done. Where do I start? Is there a right order for doing things? What professionals do I need? Not knowing is a barrier. And, without a clear path forward it's easier to do nothing. Maybe that's been your experience, too. We can only learn if we've been taught. And since we don't like to talk about death, and given the lack of guidebooks or guides, it's no wonder that we end up not doing anything.

I would have continued procrastinating except I needed to pick a topic for my thesis. Using two-birds-with-one-stone thinking, I chose to research end of life to figure out what I *need to know before I go*. The process outlined in *Good Goodbyes* is not perfect, but it will help you get started. Instead of having to reinvent the wheel, I've laid out stages and steps to make it as easy as possible. Imagine trying to put together a jigsaw puzzle without a picture. It's not impossible, but the task is much more difficult. Getting affairs in order is not as intuitive as assembling a jigsaw puzzle, but we apply that same thinking to end of life. Turn the pieces face up; find the corners; build the border; fill in the center—congratulations on making order from a jumble. And it's more fun if we work on it together.

Why Trust Me?

Personal experiences opened my eyes early to death. Over 60 years ago, I was a 4-year-old when my favorite uncle drowned in the Harlem River. My brothers and I were kept in the dark about what had happened to Uncle Brendan, although as it turns out, no one knew or ever found out. I absorbed the grief, chaos, and secrecy that seemed to surround his death. He was gone, but a holy ghost lingered. Twenty years later, my mother died. It seemed like a delayed reaction; her brother's death had broken her heart and it never healed. Several years after that, disabling injuries from a parachute accident ended my Army career and eventually led me to work as a hospital chaplain. Circumstances forced me to confront end of life early. I want to use my experiences to be your *guide at the side*, sharing what I've learned to help you.

Books on this topic are mostly written by physicians, which makes sense given the outsized role medicine plays in dying. I'm not a doctor, lawyer, or financial planner, credentials that people tend to associate with end-of-life. So why trust me? *Good Goodbyes* attempts to distill my insights and observations from the front lines of trauma and death. I may not have an MD or JD, but I have street cred from being ministered to as a patient, dealing with family member deaths, and from patients and families encountered as a chaplain – each situation wrenching, distressing, and confusing in their own ways.

What This Book Is and Isn't

Few expect illness, injury, or death. A lack of planning compounds the trauma of ER or ICU patients, whose concerns range from the mundane (who will walk and feed my dog while I'm hospitalized?) to existential (how long would I want to be kept alive on machines?).

Not everyone has a pet, but we all face an expiration date.

This book takes a strategic perspective on life's final phase, looking at the forest not trees—patterns and trends, rather than the specifics of your particular situation.

Reading is not enough. Use *Good Goodbyes* like a workbook. You have to move from awareness to action, by asking yourself hard questions and making decisions ahead of time, so you or someone else can implement the plan during a crisis. Consider, contemplate, and complete: discern what's important. Reflect on your preferences. Assemble necessary documents. And, make sure your trusted people know who they are, what you want, and where to find things. End of life is an area where surprises and secrets are not good. From your head through your hands to your heart, this is about doing the hard work of planning and preparing.

Disclaimer: *Good Goodbyes* is for informational purposes only and intended to give you the big picture. Don't rely on this book for medical, legal, or financial advice. Consult your trusted advisors about particulars or symptoms. But remember that these professionals see through the lens of their training, whether body parts, legal documents, or your net worth.

Where Do I Start?

There is no one right way. The only mistake is not doing. With that in mind, choose an entry point that fits best, based on the organizing framework of **Aware, Prepare, Share** and **Care**:

- **Aware** speaks to head wisdom: "I'm a thinker and planner. I need to wrap my head around facts first and understand what I'm dealing with before I tackle the nuts-and-bolts work." Aware gives an overview of the end-of-life landscape and landmarks on the journey – facts of life about the end of life.

- **Prepare** takes a hands-on perspective, laying out the practical applications: "I'm a doer. I want to get my house in order by taking care of the chores that will ease my family's burden." Working through these steps is a labor of love.
  - Medical ∞ The End Starts Here
  - Legal ∞ Clear the Heir-Way
  - Wealth ∞ Good Stewardship
  - Stuff ∞ Lighten Up
  - Transition ∞ On Our Own Terms
  - Disposition ∞ I'm Dead, Now What?
  - Digital ∞ Virtual Immortality

- **Share** and **Care** sections take a heart-centered approach: "Because of love, I am willing to do what it takes to have my affairs in order. It scares me, but I don't want to be a source of pain. I realize the work is not done until I communicate my values, preferences, and where things are. I share because I care." Meaning well is not enough. Being clear is kindness. Remember: sharing information with your nearest and dearest pays love forward. When it feels hard, keep love in mind as the bottom line.

- **Spirit/whole/soul** recognizes the fullness of life: Dying is a spiritual transition encompassing physical, emotional, and practical aspects. End of life can be a rite of passage rather than a medical crisis. Your illness or injury may be unavoidable, but it's a final act of will to ensure it's not the only thing. If you believe we are more than bodies, here's a chance to personalize your passage by taking a holistic approach.

Words are good; actions are better. Possibly you already know your days are numbered. If that's the case, do what you can, wherever you are in the process. Something is better than nothing and sooner is better than later. You have an opportunity to challenge the status quo by anticipating and planning, instead of waiting until you get knocked off your feet. Face the possibilities and deal with the probabilities. Because, sooner or later, the outcome is certain and the Reaper will come calling.

Your Packing List: Practicalities of Process

As I walk past the local fire station in the morning, I watch the incoming shift checking equipment. Do the engine lights work? Are the hoses rolled neatly and packed for easy removal? Is personal gear prepped and ready? If you call 911, you want the medical technician showing up with the aid bag packed, not missing essential meds. You don't want an ambulance stalling because it's run out of gas. Different gear but same routine for moms, vacationers, or paratroopers. You don't wait until the last minute to make sure your bag has the right stuff. Forget a bottle, diaper, or special blankie, and your baby will howl his unhappiness.

Pack the bag ahead of time. Fix the roof while the sun is shining. Be proactive, not reactive. The end-of-life journey is no joke – it's physically, emotionally, and practically demanding. And it's already started; we're just not exactly sure where we are on the path. Especially if you've reached a significant age milestone or are dealing with a terminal illness, collecting your thoughts and gathering documents are even more urgent. What you pack can make or break your trip, whether you're heading out on a day hike, a week at the beach, or your life journey. Personalize based on your needs. Just like skiing or boating requires different gear, you decide what information applies to you. As we work through the fraught process of contemplating life's ending, some essentials will smooth the process.

Choose a buddy: An accountability partner can help with motivation. End-of-life planning is important but usually not urgent. Tomorrow always seems like a better time to start. This is a tough topic with a big payoff. Find a supportive partner – someone who understands the importance and will hold your feet to the fire. It's easy to get sidetracked. Watching reruns or even organizing a sock drawer or alphabetizing spices have more appeal than facing the end. Choose a friend who is willing to hold your hand while you ponder imponderables, explore the mystery that awaits, and ensure your family isn't blindsided when life happens. Be prepared to be uncomfortable talking about a taboo topic and doing the tedious work. Remember your bottom line—love—and the beneficiaries of your work—your loved ones.

Find a container: Take time to find a home (physical and/or digital) for storing important documents and tangible assets. It doesn't need to be pretty, just functional. Unless you already have another system in place, find a box as a landing place to store important papers. Think of this as your treasure chest. You can decide later if you want a nicer alternative. Saving your work to the computer allows for easier updates.

Leave a map: Like a pirate with buried booty, draw a map so survivors can find your treasures. You've done the hard work; make sure it pays off. Let your loved ones know your wishes and that they can find your "treasures," whether documents, jewelry, or the location of a storage unit or safe deposit box. Talk about it. Once is not enough.

And finally, remember: timing is everything. You don't know how much warning you'll get. Have your "go-bag" packed and ready.

Conclusion: Your Love Letter to the Future

Does everything have a silver lining? Maybe. For me, getting hit by a bus in 2017 was also the catalyst for finding a thesis topic. Given the choice, I wouldn't have picked that particular experience.

But, it awakened me to mortality…

And our ultimate fragility…

And not knowing what the future holds.

It forced me to ask: was I ready if something happened – or would I be leaving a mess behind? This question keeps nagging.

What about you? Are you ready?

We don't expect to become disabled or develop dementia. It *may* happen.

Dying on the other hand? It's a *sure* thing.

If you love someone…

Or someone loves you…

DON'T WAIT.

Do it while you can. "Because of my love for you, I am handling these details. In my dying times and the aftermath of my death, you will know that I care." Start today – the first day of the rest of your life – and take the steps that will bring you peace and ease the burden on your family.

If you're convinced and ready, set your intention. The process of building a holistic foundation for your *Good Goodbye* won't be easy. But with love as the bottom line, it will be worthwhile.

Two:

Spirit

∞

Fullness of Life

The way to God is through darkness. *Let there be light.*

Kay reminisced about meeting George, the man who became her husband. They were on a double date, with different people, at Disneyland. George took her hand to hurry her across Main Street as the trolley approached. As their palms connected, Kay felt a surge of energy pass between them. It was unlike anything she had ever experienced. After several more double dates together, with George accompanied by a different person each time, he (finally) asked Kay if she would care to go out with him… They connected, married, and had two daughters. Years later, when George was diagnosed with a terminal pulmonary disease, Kay was by his side. In the hospice facility, Kay was holding George's hand when a surge went through her hand – the same spark of energy she had felt thirty-five years earlier. As the feeling subsided, George stopped breathing.

The Great Unknown

"Everybody wants to go to heaven, but nobody wants to die."[6]

What comes next after this earthly existence: heaven, hell, or oblivion? When we die, are we just gone? Is there really a heaven up there and a hell down there? Your guess is as good as mine. Facing what happens next is a legitimate concern. Americans have strong views: around 72% believe in heaven and 58% believe in hell,[7] with percentages even higher for Christians. Paradoxically, although most Americans believe in an afterlife, they fear passage to eternity and the celestial future that awaits.

One of the selling points for embracing a particular religion is expedited entry to the "good" place – a heavenly EZ Pass. While involvement with a religion includes many benefits, by itself, going to church doesn't make you "good" any more than going to a garage makes you a car. Terror about the unknown can keep people hurtling along a *do everything* medical track. We trust the devil we know, the *here and now*, even with its difficulties and limitations. The lack of customer reviews on the afterlife, peer-reviewed studies on heaven, or a navigation device for reaching that destination means that many of us cope with our deep-seated fear of death by denying or ignoring what's ahead. Some who have survived near-death experiences describe a tunnel leading to light and encountering a welcoming presence. I imagine the transition as more like a water slide. Zipping down an exhilarating, scary, and unstoppable ride until – surprise! A splash, soft landing, and embrace by warm water. Someday, we'll find out… Perhaps upon arrival, we will have a feeling of déjà vu: "I remember this place. I'm home."[8]

All are Spiritual; Some are Religious

"There is no religion without love, and people may talk as much as they like about their religion, but if it does not teach them to be good and kind to man and beast, it is all a sham."[9]

Not everyone embraces formal religion, which focuses on particular beliefs, rituals, and practices. It doesn't matter. The existential aspect of life is holistic and universal, integrating body, mind, and spirit. Our biological presence is merely a vessel for essence. If human existence is more than physical, it follows that our living and dying are also more than medical events. Soul escapes detection by experienced practitioner, physical exam, or diagnostic test. Whether this intangible aspect survives the dissolution of the body depends on whether you ask a physician or a philosopher. Father Teilhard de Chardin suggests, "We are not human beings having a spiritual experience. We are spiritual beings having a human experience."[10] *Spiritual* derives from Latin *spiritus* meaning *breath*, a root also shared with words like *inspiration, respiration,* and *expiration.* If we have breath, we have a spiritual core, whether or not we follow a particular religious tradition. Spirit is the essential, animating, vital core in the center of our being. Spirituality is about the sacred, encompassing relationships, meaning, and purpose. Our physical bodies meet the definition of sacramental – an outward sign of inward grace.

   In the U.S., religion is culturally embedded[11]: Christmas is a federal holiday, citizens recite "one nation under God" in the Pledge of Allegiance, "In God We Trust" appears on money, and elected officials and witnesses in a court of law often swear on a Bible. Eighty percent of U.S. adults believe in God, even if not the God described in the Bible.[12] Seventy percent of Americans identify as Christian.[13] While religion seems to imply participation in communal practices, not all who claim to be Christian are affiliated with a church or observant of denominational duties.[14]

Whether we consider ourselves religious or not, eventually we face mortality – our ultimate reality – an existential endeavor with spiritual aspects. Dying well isn't a matter of the right medicine, procedure, or doctor; a good death becomes more likely when one has lived a life of purpose and connection, acknowledging that physical bodies expire. The current medical norm primarily focuses on bodily death. However, accepting death as a natural boundary can offer clarity about what does and doesn't matter.

The obsession with biological functioning and clinical outcomes overlooks the possibility of opening to spiritual essence. Often, we forsake delving into life's big questions until loss or trauma forces us to pay attention. At such times, recognizing a common spiritual bond can connect us with fellow seekers and catalyze changes. Instead of or in addition to following a religion, many Americans believe in healthcare, deifying doctors not only as medical authorities, but elevated to a priestly caste of miracle workers.

Embracing Change

"All endings are also beginnings; we just don't know it at the time."[15]

If a pregnant woman showed up in the ER without having acknowledged her condition, had prenatal care, or collected essentials for her newborn, would that seem normal or odd? The secrecy and lack of planning would affect not only the new mother but also the baby and any who step in to try to help the family cope. Most women prepare, at least minimally, before giving birth.

Why do we treat dying so differently? Loss is part of life. Growth means change, bringing opportunities and costs. When a crawling baby learns to walk, she leaves infancy behind for toddlerhood. Mobility brings more freedom for the baby but also requires caregivers to adapt with improved safety precautions. Aging brings changes, both physically and socially. During post-employment years, individuals enter a new phase, leaving jobs and eventually qualifying for Medicare and Social Security. However, people are mostly on their own navigating this new terrain. Except for a lucky few honored at a retirement party, no rite commemorates this passage. But more than just a ceremony, we need guidebooks, mentors, and workshops to provide instruction. We rightly assume resources will be available to help us navigate other significant changes earlier in our lives, such as having a baby or getting married. With longer life, many people will live for decades after employment, and yet elder years are relatively uncharted territory, like the "Here be dragons" notation on medieval maps. Hope seems to be our approach for the final stage of life's journey.

A life of integrity is a continuing endeavor – seeking wholeness and embracing all developmental stages. The sense of urgency grows as time gets shorter. Psychologist Erik Erikson's model of human development divides the lifespan into eight stages.[16] Around ages 40+, adults struggle with questions of generativity or stagnation. Did my life have meaning? How did I make a difference? How does my life fit into the big picture?

In the final stage of Erikson's model occurring around ages 65+, the conflict is between reconciling integrity versus despair. Looking back on life and pondering whether I lived up to my soul's purpose for being can lead to a sense of satisfaction or regrets.

Touchstones

Who and what are most important to you? Understand what you believe is your personal guidance system, your North Star. Being clear about your values and what you consider right and wrong provide a touchstone for decision-making as you consider end-of-life preferences. Ethics are how we act on our values. Autonomy, competence, and relatedness are foundational human needs, according to psychologists. As we move from childhood to adulthood, we grow in the ability to fulfill these needs. Autonomy is the degree to which you feel a sense of agency and responsibility for your behaviors. Competence relates to capabilities and feelings of being effective. Relatedness is a sense of belonging and connection to others.[17] We tend to act in ways that lead to the outcomes we desire. Humans are naturally inclined to grow; however, at a certain point, it's likely that autonomy, relatedness, and competence will trend downward. You're the only one who knows your values, but don't keep them a secret. Let others know in case they end up as your surrogate decision-maker. The planning part is still going...

Doctors expect patients to make intelligent decisions, which assumes autonomy and competence. Capacity to choose competently rests on your ability to understand what a certain procedure entails. Starting in the 1960s, pregnancy and delivery became more patient-centered. Within several generations, childbirth changed from a doctor-centered, mother-sedated, father-excluded medical event to a holistic experience where parents develop detailed birthing plans with customized prefer-ences. From a bygone era of a professional deciding about mothers' best interests, women now expect to be in control of their birth experience. As much as the phrase "My body, my choices" has been demonized, it summarizes the core principle of patient autonomy. Who is the boss of your body?

As it is at the beginning, so it can be at the end. It's your body, your life, and your dying. Will you control the controllables or cede your power and independence by not planning? You have the right to decide about care, but this requires planning in advance and having documents completed and available when needed.[18] You have both rights and responsibilities. Failing to take action and make decisions about health care preferences undermines autonomy and transfers the burden to someone else.

In the event of incapacitation, you entrust someone else to make decisions. Who will play God for you? If you want autonomy and the freedom to choose, you need to expect and plan for death. Failing to anticipate guarantees hitching a ride on the medical express train, some-times to the end of the line. Determining preferences ahead of time and alerting others about those wishes reduces stress for decision makers if a patient cannot communicate. This also allows the health care team to concentrate resources appropriately based on the whole picture.

At the heart of spirituality is integration—the prospect of wholeness instead of fragmentation. While crisis can catalyze transformation, circumstances do not always allow time to change course. Each of us needs to live true to whom we are – preferably before getting sick, before encountering the reality of ultimate outcome, and before being forced to deal with unrelenting effects of illness and treatment. Humans cannot avoid death, but we can control the dying process.

Spirituality in Practice

Michelangelo's painting of the "Creation of Adam" shows God and Adam reaching towards one another, with arms outstretched and index fingers almost touching. A surge of energy seems to flow from God to human, kindling life into being. Every breath we take provides the opportunity for inspiration. On the journey through life, engaging regularly in spiritual practices, such as lighting a candle or saying grace, can cultivate self-awareness and encourage joy. Done with intention, many everyday disciplines such as meditation, prayer, journaling, gardening, or movement can help us to wake up. When we're in touch with something greater and balancing inspiration with expression, the grace we receive can become a source of healing for others.

Immortality

- Have you thought through the idea of living forever?
- Would you want life without end, with a body that inevitably declines?
- Or if you were immortal, would you want to live if the people you love died?
- How do you see yourself spending unlimited time alive, especially if you're apt to complain, "There's nothing to do!" on a rainy weekend or when the internet and cable are out?

While death tends to be viewed as enemy, would we really want to live without end? It's an academic question. Unfortunately, or perhaps fortunately, immortality is mythical. Jonathan Swift explored the idea in his novel *Gulliver's Travels*. Special humans—the Struldbrugs—are eternal. Here's the catch: while they do not die, they continue aging.[19] Our fears about death would presume that *not* dying is preferable. But at a certain point, living has adverse side effects such as declining vigor and increasing dependency. Be careful what you wish for... Living forever may be more a curse than a blessing.

Conclusion: Live Life to the Fullest

"Unless a grain of wheat falls into the earth and dies, it remains alone; but if it dies, it bears much fruit."[20]

During the last few weeks of Mimi's life, she spent a lot of time in bed with her eyes closed and not very lucid or responsive. Mimi had grown up listening to opera; her mother would sing arias to her. On the last three visits by her daughter, they listened to Mimi's favorite music: opera and hymns. During Jussi Björling's rendition of "Santa Lucia," Mimi sang along with the recording loudly and clearly and invited her daughter to sing along too. Mimi sang and cried. The crying concerned her daughter who asked if she was okay. She responded: "It's so beautiful." The same thing happened on the next two visits – the singing, the crying, and exclaiming "It's so beautiful." On the day leading up to the third occasion, Mimi had been very quiet. She and her daughter sang and listened to hymns. When Mimi's granddaughter visited, Katie reminded Mimi of their special song. They sang "Red, Red Robin" together, cried, and said their good-byes. In the middle of the night, Mimi started singing "Santa Lucia" very loudly. Her daughter asked her to be quiet. Mimi complied, but then started singing again. This went on until almost dawn. During the day, she complained about back pain and received her first and only dose of morphine. When her daughter stopped by that evening, Mimi was sleeping. Dolphy kissed her, said "I love you," and went home. Early the next morning, Mimi passed into eternal life.

Is death a limiting constraint or liberating force? Life has boundaries. Knowing that our life will come to an end can give a sense of urgency. Death can free us from inertia and rouse us to action. Confronting the reality and inevitability of our final passage is a vital challenge for humans. It necessitates that we acknowledge our eventual date with destiny, while at the same time befriending the ambiguities and mystery this transition promises. To face death courageously is to reclaim our last rights and begin to make peace with mortality.

Reflections:

- What feeds my soul or makes my spirit sing?
- What practices help keep my spiritual compass true?
- What do I want people to remember about me?
- What legacy do I want to leave for future generations?
- What did life reveal to me? What did I come to see or know clearly?
- What am I living for?

Actions:

- Choose a spiritual discipline that resonates. Try some different ones, like writing haiku, watercolor painting, or working with clay.
- Keep a gratitude journal where you record your daily thankfuls. Share with a loved one.

- Set a timer for five minutes to sit quietly. Record ideas and blessings in a notebook.
- Compile a "bucket" list of goals, dreams, and aspirations you want to achieve while you are alive.

Resources:

- Religious views on end-of-life https://www.pewforum.org/2013/11/21/religious-groups-views-on-end-of-life-issues/
- Religious views on death https://www.uofazcenteronaging.com/care-sheet/providers/religion-and-end-life-part-1-how-different-religions-view-end-life

THREE:

AWARE

∞

THE FACTS OF LIFE ABOUT THE END OF LIFE

Things fall apart; the centre cannot hold;
Mere anarchy is loosed upon the world. ~W.B. Yeats

Chaplains might get called to any area of the hospital for someone who is having a bad day. Pediatric patients are the hardest, like the two-year-old who choked on a mouthful of peanuts. His parents sat in shock at their little boy's bedside awaiting surgery to harvest his organs. Or another two-year-old who had wandered into a swimming pool. His body survived the submersion, but not his brain, although he lived for several years afterward. And then, some situations left me shaking my head, like being paged to the neurological ICU to be with a family as doctors delivered bad news. Tests were conclusive; the patient was brain dead and not going to survive the stroke that caused her hospitalization. Her distraught daughter cried, "It's too soon!" The patient was 85 years old.

Is there an appropriate age to die? Is it always too soon? Is it sometimes too late? When is "just right"? Death may seem random but it's predictable; maybe shocking, but not surprising. We may get a postponement, but no exemptions are granted. Not everyone will get pregnant, but everyone who has been born will die. The natural order may be unwelcome, but there's no escaping it. Life ends; the beginning is also the beginning of the end. It's hard to conceive of not being. But sticking our heads in the sand doesn't mean that death won't find us. The problem is that since we don't talk about dying, when it does arrive just means we feel ambushed and unprepared. Pretending and avoiding do not serve us well. Kudos for having the courage to face this cultural taboo.

The Great Delusion: The Lies We Tell Ourselves

"We can run, but we can't hide."[21]

Because we don't face reality or wait until we get waylaid, we can make it harder on ourselves and our families. A foundational myth is that we will be safe, or if not, medicine will save us. Other myths and facts about life:

Myth: Death is an aberration.
Fact: Death is the last phase of life.

Myth: We can avoid death.
Fact: Like sunset follows sunrise, death follows birth.

Myth: Dying is solely a medical event supervised by professional providers.
Fact: Like pregnancy, life's end is more than a medical event.

Myth: Death is an ambush.
Fact: The death rate is 100%. By age sixty-five, a limited number of diagnoses will cause death as the Wheel of Fortune displays.

Myth: With the right treatment and care, many patients will live forever.
Fact: All "saves" are temporary.

Myth: Most people will die in their sleep.
Fact: Around 90% of elderly people (over ages 65+) eventually die of chronic illnesses after a declining trajectory that can last years.

We have certain expectations about how life will end. For the most part, they're wrong. One mistaken belief is that doctors will guide us through the final transition. We forget that doctors are scientists, often focused on a very specialized part of the body, such as the surgeon who informed me: "I'm a hand doctor. I don't treat anything above the elbow." Doctors, who don't want to upset patients, will offer treatments because something is better than nothing, overlooking that medical care is intended as a bridge back to health and functioning. Not knowing the facts may find some tethered to "life" support in an intensive care unit or families who they want "everything done" for a loved one without realizing the pain, suffering, and cost that "everything" will entail. We can fool ourselves some of the time, but we don't get out alive, no matter how much we pretend, ignore, or deny.

Alive Versus Living: What Lies Ahead

We're born; we live; we die. Death isn't separate from life; it's an inevitable consequence of being born. Naming a thing is an essential first step to understanding it. Words like *life* and *living* are used automatically, often triggering an emotional response, especially when it concerns a loved one or aligns with a strongly held viewpoint. But what exactly does *alive* mean? Is alive/dead a binary, like an on/off switch? Can someone be alive and yet not living? What might that look like? Is living a continuum, where some displays represent vital signs, while other indicators measure vitality signs, such as relationships, autonomy, and purpose?

Except that our system only tracks vital signs, not vitality signs, because the medical domain primarily focuses on biological functioning. Measuring numbers is easy: blood pressure, temperature, respiration, pulse, and urine output. Do these numbers constitute life? Advances in medical technology and pharmaceuticals mean that bodies can be kept "alive" that otherwise wouldn't survive. Sometimes, ventilators and feeding tubes can allow time for healing and serve as a bridge back to health. But as it turns out, certain functions can be maintained for lengthy periods, even in the absence of brain activity. Does death occur when a *person* ceases to be, or when the *body* stops functioning? Life "saving" technology has distorted the boundary. Individuals and society must grapple with the life/death distinction because not only does lifespan often exceed health span, but there are times when the body continues operating even though the resident has vacated the premises. People may enter pre-mortem limbo, a state of existence without consciousness, that affects not only the person experiencing illness or dementia but also caregivers.

With modern medicine blurring the line, the law stepped in to delineate the life/death boundary, although always lagging behind ever-evolving existence-prolonging medical care. Identifying when death occurs has important implications, such as for organ donation. A sliding scale differentiates coma or persistent vegetative state (PVS) from brain death. The 1981 Uniform Determination of Death Act established two specific legal criteria for death: "Irreversible cessation of circulatory and respiratory functions, (or) irreversible cessation of all functions of the entire brain, including the brain stem."[22] Heart, lungs, and brain – and the greatest of these is the brain.

A Date with Fate: Calculating Your "Done" Date

Nothing in life is to be feared, it is only to be understood. Now is the time to understand more, so that we may fear less.[23]

"Tell me, Doc. How long do I have?" Your physician won't be able to give an exact answer. Death may be the clinical event everyone will experience, but life's conclusion is harder to determine than a baby's due date. It's also a discussion many doctors would rather avoid unless a patient initiates a conversation.

We aren't statistics, but data and trends can give a sense of how the end will come. According to the Centers for Disease Control and Prevention (CDC), life expectancy in the United States (pre-COVID) was 78.8 years.[24] But, that's a guess and an average, more than a target. Life expectancy is like car advertising: "actual mileage may vary."

Variables such as race, gender, ethnicity,[25] and now COVID, have an influence. So do some things over which we have control, such as eating habits, exercising, and whether we tempt fate by engaging in risky behaviors, like smoking or riding a motorcycle unhelmeted. And there are always chance encounters, like getting hit by a bus, that might revise estimates.

For planning purposes, we can round up our approximate life expectancy to 80 years. To get a ballpark figure for Time Remaining (TR)[26], subtract your current age from 80. The difference is the number of years remaining (or borrowed time, if you're over 80). "What? Wait, this is how many years I have left? No way. I've always been above-average." This simple math problem may rattle the psyche, or we can choose to ignore it because it's only a rough estimate. But it may also jolt you into working on your bucket list. For a more specific figure, use the Social Security Administration's Life Expectancy[27] calculator. While it's good to remember that we're individuals, not statistics, but also don't forget every day we're a bit closer to the end. Things will fall apart. We just don't know when, where, or how.

Lifespan: It's Not Just About Age

Your age is just a number. It doesn't account for health, connections, or meaning. Health span indicates the period of life during which a person is generally healthy and free from serious illnesses. Quality of life correlates with health. A gap between lifespan and health span may be filled with prolonged pain, suffering, or insentience. While health care advances have extended age, the extra years get tacked on at the end. Sometimes living longer means more debility. You might think of the gap between Life Expectancy (LE) and Health Adjusted Life Expectancy (HALE) as the difference between quantity and quality. Age without wellness might be more than you bargained for.

Forecasting the End: The Wheel of Fortune

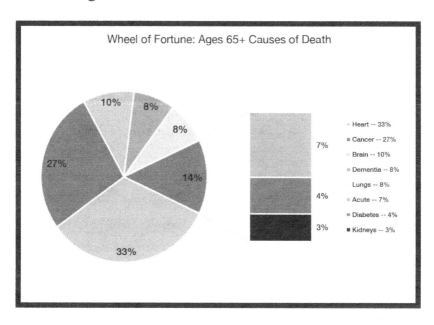

Figure 1: Causes of death in US for ages 65+ [28]

How will it all end? It's not voodoo. Once a person is born, the eventual outcome is destined, just not how or when. There are limited possibilities for those ages 65 and older. Hundreds of diagnoses fall into eight main causes of death. Biological functioning is multifaceted and interconnected; however, ultimately, cascading effects will cause the failure of three vital organs—heart, lungs, and/or brain—which results in death.

Forecasting the future is like spinning a wheel of fortune. Where will the wheel stop? What will eventually kill me? The process isn't completely random, but instead based on an individual's personal habits, family history, and biological weak link. Over a lifetime, the range of possibilities narrows. Trends in mortality have changed in the past 100 years; infectious diseases shifted to chronic illnesses (e.g., cardiovascular disease, cancer, and stroke) as the most common causes of death. Until COVID… COVID-19 became the third leading cause of death in 2020[29] after cancer and heart disease. Some predict that the gains made in average lifespan may be declining, not only because of infectious diseases, but also because of obesity, with its collateral damage.[30]

Among Americans over the age of sixty-five, a third (33%) will die from heart ailments while another 27% succumb to cancer and its side effects. Seven chronic diseases (heart failure 33%, cancer 27%, pulmonary disease 8%, neurological injuries 10%, dementia 6%, diabetes 4%, and kidney disease 3%) account for 93 percent of the deaths for this age cohort.[31] While there is usually no single cause for death, contributing factors include disease, genetics, and personal behaviors. For example, obesity can cause multiple, serious health complications such as heart disease, diabetes, and/or cancer: "As the defects in a complex system increase, the time comes when just one more defect is enough to impair the whole."[32]

The term *sudden* generally refers to death resulting from trauma, a cardiopulmonary or neurological event, massive systemic infection, or influenza. *Sudden* doesn't mean unexpected. While in some cases the death occurs abruptly, after a certain age, decline and a constellation of chronic conditions have set the stage for an acute episode from which a patient cannot recover.

A facilitator opened a Death Café[33] session with an icebreaker: "How do you want to die?" In many settings, a question like that would freeze rather than spark conversation given the superstitions attached to mentioning death. Although most adults realize that saying something doesn't create it, we make an exception for magical thinking about death – *that which must not be named*. Most Death Café participants preferred "dying in sleep"—*sudden death*—going to sleep and not waking up. This acute scenario entails full functioning until being launched over a metaphorical waterfall. However, statistically only 7% of age 65+ adults will die suddenly, as a result of trauma such as falls, or from flu, pneumonia, or infection.[34] And for some, they have also been dealing with significant underlying health issues already until an infection causes them to die "suddenly."

The situation more of us are likely to encounter is a gradual decline of function from multiple underlying illnesses or co-morbidities of the heart, lungs, or brain (stroke or dementia), or from cancer or diabetes. After age 65, most deaths will correspond to a slow fade, a declining trajectory of loss of functioning over time.[35] Many progressive illnesses such as cancer, organ failure, frailty, or dementia involve long periods of deterioration, aggravated by intermittent acute episodes. A frail elder will experience prolonged diminishment as a result of brain trauma, cognitive incapacity, or multiple organ failure before "The End." Declining functioning is inversely related to caregiving needs. The less you can do for yourself, the more help you need.

It doesn't take a crystal ball. At a certain age, the downward slope for over 90% of us is gradual but inexorable. Rather than a waterfall, dying will be more like a riptide, superficially benign and invisibly treacherous.

Individually insignificant maladies will accumulate to knock us over, resulting in less stamina, more medicines, periodic hospitalizations, and a dance card filled with doctor visits. Contributing factors such as disease, genetics, medications, and behaviors help forecast a likely cause of death. Additionally, chronic ailments and limited mobility make people more susceptible to infections.

One of the more unforgettable incidents I observed as a chaplain was watching an older woman receive cardiopulmonary resuscitation (CPR) three times over the course of eight hours. Twice she was resuscitated. Death ultimately won, but not without a fight from the code team. Before the attending physician instructed the team to stop, the woman's abdominal area looked like a trampoline. With each chest compression, her stomach heaved and sloshed. If not for the hospital room and white coats, what happened looked a lot like torture.

CPR is not like what you see on TV. Risks from CPR include potential for rib fractures, internal organ trauma, and permanent neurological damage.[36] In-hospital success rate for CPR varies, ranging from 15% for those under age 70 to 0% at ages over 89. One conundrum: the most successful CPR occurs when someone is hospitalized, which indicates some affiliated illness or injury. And how is success defined? Obviously, it would be restoration of a heart rhythm, but what does that mean for the patient—survival for 24 hours, discharge from the hospital to a custodial care facility, or regaining functionality? There are no consistent criteria; standards vary by facility. Although around 73% percent of the post-CPR deaths occur within 72 hours, sometimes successfully resuscitated patients have permanent neurological impairments.[37] The *Wall Street Journal* reported on a 2010 study of more than 95,000 cases of CPR which found that only 8% of patients survived for more than one month.[38] Of these, only about 3% could lead a mostly normal life. Despite these statistics, the standard of care requires CPR, without regard for age or underlying disease.

Notwithstanding technological advances that extend body functioning, death ultimately comes. Unless someone concedes that death is part of the human condition, there is no reason to change how we approach end of life. Awareness of reality allows the ability to frame dying in alignment with values. Many people have misconceptions about the effectiveness of procedures. Examples of interventions shown in the media deceive by looking routine, easy, and reliable. On the contrary, someone who undergoes chest compressions heads to an ICU, not sauntering out of the hospital, seemingly little worse for the wear after getting pummeled.

Healing Versus Curing

"Dying is something we human beings do continuously, not just at the end of our physical lives on this earth."[39]

Often people use the words *healing* and *curing* interchangeably. There's a subtle difference: Healing is possible without curing and curing without healing. Healing comes from the Old English hǣlan and means "restore to sound health or make whole."[40] Cure has the Latin root *curare,* "take care of" or "treat medically,"[41] providing a substance or procedure that relieves a disease or condition. Generally, the word "cure" is specific, whereas healing is holistic. A treatment administered may lead to a cure and eradicate illness; healing is transformational and wholeness-enhancing. As an example, unless a patient with Type 2 diabetes also engages in healing activities, such as changing eating and exercise habits, the cure is a Band-Aid®. Our current health care system mostly emphasizes curing, often absolving patients of responsibility to participate in their return to health.

Particularly at end-of-life, the focus is on curing the body, without considering the whole human, which includes not only the individual patient, but others affected by illness – loved ones and caregivers. Hospice takes the family system into account with its comprehensive approach; however, rules impose limits so many patients don't enroll until late in the disease process.

How much does matter matter? Are we human because of matter or spirit? Nature teaches that energy is conserved even when it changes form – gas, water, solid. This truism also applies to humans. When the solid body "dies," perhaps we are engaged in a phase change. Because of its undetectable nature, we disregard life's through-line – soul – an eternal element that defines us as human and survives bodily termination. Life's big questions—Did we exist before incarnating? Will we exist after death?—are existential, not empirical. And the answers are not so much a matter of evidence but of belief. While scientifically unprovable, the temporal body seems to house a perpetual light, which is how we know about deceased luminaries, such as Jesus, Shakespeare, Einstein, and Mozart, whose legacies survived mortality.

Person or Patient?

The existing medical system is paradoxical, supposedly for the good of patients, but operating with doctors, treatments, and technology as lead actors in an unfolding medical drama where energy is directed towards curing without considering healing. Patients play bit parts – objects being done to. But patients are also complicit with the system, often going along without questioning. It takes courage to face the end and say, "Enough." If someone does not or cannot insist on being addressed in full personhood, the individual will continue to be viewed and treated as a collection of malfunctioning body parts, rather than as a whole person.

Twentieth century inventions have increased the medicalization of end of life. Advances have been a boon, but technology has assumed an outsized role in health care, particularly at end-of-life. Originally, machines were intended to provide temporary support while underlying disease resolved, such as iron lungs used by polio sufferers while recovering from the virus. The health care system has adopted mandatory procedures like CPR, regardless of underlying conditions that would thwart successful outcomes. The pendulum has swung so that technological interventions are the default, regardless of efficacy. Indiscriminate use of a high-tech approach may cause more suffering for patients and can raise ethical questions regarding the intent of treatment.

Patients trust that their best interests motivate those who are providing care. However, illiteracy about aging and lack of full disclosure may lead to faulty expectations about success rates for procedures. Prevalence presumes usefulness, like administering CPR. Informed consent requires that people prepare ahead of time and weigh what is more important: to be a patient or person. Am I a body, or do I have a body? Is curing more important than healing? It's easier to fix a broken bone or track the alive/dead binary than to monitor or promote well-being. So naturally, the medical establishment often directs resources at things that can be repaired or measured.

Many patients don't ask and physicians don't tell. Patients assume that if a doctor recommends a treatment, it is in their best interests to accept that protocol. They acquiesce, without awareness of the full gamut of side effects, financial burden, risks, or whether they will even benefit. Failing to confront reality has its own side-effects. In taking a medical history, many physicians don't ask about values and what things are most important to patients. Their responsibility ends with diagnosing and treating ailments. The health care system supports failing organs with medicine and technology rather than ensuring fullness of being. Being unbroken is not the same as being whole.

Illness Versus Disease

Disease differs from illness. Harvard Professor Arthur Kleinman explains: "Modern physicians diagnose and treat diseases (abnormalities in the structure and function of body organs and systems), whereas patients suffer illnesses (experiences of disvalued changes in states of being and in social function; the human experience of sickness)."[42] Concentrating on disease has its place, but there comes a time when *something more* does not involve procedures or drugs. Dr. Gawande reminds:

> "Good medical care can influence the direction a person's old age will take. Most of us in medicine, however, don't know how to think about decline. We're good at addressing specific, individual problems: colon cancer, high blood pressure, arthritic knees. Give us a disease, and we can do something about it."[43]

Planning for aging requires balancing spiritual and practical preparation, hope and realism, and knowing life has meaning even though it ends. Having faith that something exists beyond the cessation of vital signs requires reviewing one's life; completing essential tasks; and being confident that we will be okay, just as we were before we were born. There comes a time to recognize that the battle can't be won, that return to a meaningful life is not an option, and to promote measures that enhance quality over quantity of life.

Defining life, deciding about death, and determining what treatments are appropriate goes beyond I-know-it-when-I-see-it. Medicine, law, religion, as well as concerned family members, will all weigh in to figure out what life means and when it ends, what kind of life a person might want, how to differentiate between extending life or prolonging death, and to distinguish between ordinary versus extraordinary treatments. Unless a nursing home bed is where you'd like to spend years, or possibly decades of your life, understand that a little planning and documentation can go a long way. Heed the cautionary tales of others to avoid subjecting those you love to turmoil and discord.

Conclusion

Reality is the leading cause of stress among those in touch with it.[44]

If you stand outside any hospital, heartbreak is taking place inside behind that facade. What did you think would happen? Even when expected for a patient enrolled in hospice, the end of a life can take us by surprise. To minimize the shock, remember this: living begets dying; it's a numbers game based on the wheel of fortune. The older a person gets, the fewer the possibilities for how death will show up. The course of diseases and the aging process have predictable elements, though individual experiences vary and may diverge from expectations or statistics. The reality is that humans have a *deadline* and all "saves" are temporary. Eventually, we get the Humpty Dumpty outcome.

Take a deep breath. Accept the reality of what is. It's beyond our control. Do not rely on optimistic expectations alone. Understanding what you may face and being smart about advance preparations will make things easier. Life is provisional. Death is inevitable. There's a time to place our faith in high-tech medicine and entrust our fate to scientists. Being older does not naturally result in being wiser or more prepared. Even those who have lived decades may fail to be ready for the transition back home. If we live with the end in mind, death can become a catalyst for achieving dreams because we are not promised tomorrow. Your destiny awaits.

Reflections:

- How do you define life? Is the body who I am or something that I temporarily occupy?
- Do you view death as a fatal flaw or a defining boundary?
- What's your line in the sand? What does being alive mean to you: vital signs or vitality signs?

Actions:

- The countdown timer started at birth. Wake up to the reality that life ends.
- Express your preferences. Provide crucial information to those you care about.
- Befriending the end requires providing information about the fate we face. Not to scare ; it's just information. Sometimes people are unaware.

Resources:

- E-book: THE FIVE TRAJECTORIES: Supporting Patients During Serious Illness https://csupalliativecare.org/wp-content/uploads/Five-Trajectories-eBook-02.21.2018.pdf

FOUR:

PREPARE

∞

A LABOR OF LOVE

"In the middle of the journey of our life I came to myself within a dark wood where the straight way was lost. ...What a wild, and rough, and stubborn wood this was, which in my thought renews the fear!"— Dante Alighieri, *The Divine Comedy*

I was recently graduated, newly married, and stationed in Germany. After an 11-month separation, my lieutenant husband had finished his Army training in the U.S. and would be joining me. On Monday of that week, my brother called: "Mom fell out of bed. She's in the hospital."

Two days later: "She's in the ICU. Doctors aren't sure what's going on."

By Friday: "Her organs are failing. She's not going to make it."

In a matter of five days, my mother's "back problems" (apparently, a cover story for a slew of underlying health issues) led to her death. After receiving the official Red Cross notification, we arranged emergency leave, and headed back to the States.

Maybe you've been shocked by the sudden death of a loved one. Perhaps you remember the visceral, churning feelings: disbelief, dizziness, shortness of breath, nausea.

We arrived in the U.S., jet-lagged and emotionally devastated. Forget bereavement; a short timeline forced us into decision-making mode. So many details to handle: a funeral to plan, a burial to arrange, belongings to claim. Bills started arriving immediately, a steady stream of expenses for doctors, hospital, and funeral. Incomprehensible invoices competed with personal condolence messages. When we finally located my parents' checkbook, their bank account was overdrawn. Now what? As the ones who had money, my husband and I paid bills.

My mother's death wasn't the first that I remember, but it was the first for which I had decision-making and financial responsibilities. And forty years later, my memories are still a complicated mess of grief, discombobulation, and frustration.

The feeling of being ambushed lingers. I've since discovered that my experiences are typical. With subsequent family deaths and watching how patients and families react and cope made me realize the universality – and insanity – of being surprised by and unprepared for death. A death often brings shock and crisis, but it's not a surprise. A family will usually pull together to solve the immediate problem, forgetting that this wake-up call will happen again. It's as if someone runs head-first into a wall and expects to *not* get hurt—repeatedly. Whether it's crashing into something, or dying, doing the same thing and expecting different results is irrational.

The first step to changing behavior is being aware. If we admit that life ends, we can be ready for when that time comes. Because the time will come. Death may be sudden; it will probably be devastating, but it's not unexpected. Hope is wonderful, but choosing to not see, hear, or speak about reality doesn't make for a great planning strategy. Unless your crystal ball is calibrated for accurate predictions, the wiser course of action would be to plan ahead. It's possible to wait. Maybe the timing will be such that you're ready on D-Day-minus-one, whether that's the day before you die or when pre-departure decline impairs decision-making capacity. We nod along with Mark Twain's sentiment: "I know that everyone dies, but I always thought an exception would be made in my case."[45] Our date with destiny is coming, even though we don't know exactly when, given humans' unfortunate lack of warning indicators signaling a low tank or battery.

When we drive, we don't expect an accident, but it might happen. Given the possibility and potential for a bad outcome, prudent people buckle a seatbelt after climbing in the car. You never know. That's the approach *Good Goodbyes* advocates with life preparations. Be mindful. Be ready. Because just-in-time may be a little-too-late.

To do or not to do, that is your choice. It's not enough to be AWARE. You have to take steps to PREPARE, building a bridge from awareness to action. "Love today! We are never promised a tomorrow."[46] But, don't just live for today; think about the impact your sudden exit would have on others.

The Prepare section will help guide you through practicalities. It's hands-on and intended to encourage you to get started. The next seven chapters and the one-page Treasure Map document (Appendix 1) will walk you through "getting affairs in order" steps. Each chapter introduces opportunities to *Learn, Reflect*, and *Act*. *Learn* provides background information – what you need to know before you go. *Reflect* has questions to inspire an examination of values. And finally, *Act*. Given the possibilities and your preferences, personalize to reflect your wishes. Because one-size-doesn't-fit-all, you decide and document. If autonomy, another word for freedom, is important, you need to let others know in advance what you'd want in certain circumstances. Act on your good intentions.

Fortune telling skills may be fun, just don't rely on magical thinking as a planning strategy. As you read the Prepare section, take what you need and ignore what doesn't fit. Do the work, because preparation is a gift for yourself and your survivors. Gathering the information your loved ones will need, clarifying what's important, and mapping the location of your treasures is a lasting legacy. Proper prior planning helps prevent prolonged pain.

Essential Prep For Life's Journey

Hiking to Phantom Ranch at the bottom of the Grand Canyon was memorable – and not just because of the view, terrain, and weather variability. The warnings before setting off were dire: "This is serious business. Some have needed rescuing. Others have died. Don't be one of them. Be prepared for the adventure ahead."

Before you embark on a vacation, you pack items to make the trip reasonably comfortable. If you've headed into the wilderness, you know that researching your destination, selecting a suitable route, and carrying the right equipment will make the experience more enjoyable and safer. Preparation can even mean the difference between survival or disaster. Not planning is a recipe for trouble.

Unlike the possibility of a hiking accident, death is a sure thing.

Dying may be universal but few give much thought to end of life, which means we're unprepared, practically and spiritually. How we die has some variability, but there are certain things every adult needs. *Good Goodbyes* is the antidote to do-it-yourself – the book helps identify the milestones we'll encounter, a process to navigate the terrain, and who to include on your team. We're all in this together and we don't need to go it alone. Being smart about advance planning can make a difference with your ability to cope and how traumatized your survivors will be. Don't rely on optimism alone. Put preparation before expiration on your to-do list.

Have discussions and get your affairs in order when dying is an abstraction, not when it's breathing down your neck. You've made up your mind to do something. Where do you start? How can you make sure your family isn't scrambling to find your papers, figure out what you might want, or host a fundraising page to raise money to pay for a funeral?

Find a Buddy

It's comforting to have a companion on a journey. This existential adventure is universal, and personal. Ask for help. Don't go it alone. An accountability partner can keep you moving in the right direction, whether it's achieving fitness goals, losing weight, or getting your end-of-life act together. If you tend to procrastinate, a partner can be the antidote. If like me, you've waited until the last minute to cram for a final exam or to file taxes, you know a deadline can motivate action. Delaying end-of-life preparation may mean we get around to it too late. The panic that comes from a doctor's advice to "get your affairs in order" may be a great motivator, but it might be a ticking time bomb with a blast that unintentionally hurts others. Don't count on having the time or capacity when you're in the midst of a crisis.

With freedom comes responsibility. Being a grown-up means anticipating and planning in order to get ahead of a predictable storm. We can postpone preparing for a hurricane and hope it misses. At least with weather, you might get lucky. Don't do that with planning for life's final phase. Like the inevitability of sunrise and sunset, our life cycle means death is coming. Forewarned is forearmed.

Packing List For Your Treasure Chest

Before you slip, trip, or fall onto the end-of-life glide path, take the time to pack. Call it your "go" bag or treasure chest – choose a name that tickles your fancy or adopt a symbolic skull and crossbones. Find a container, which will be the landing zone for storing important documents as you collect them. If you have an existing system, you're already ahead of the game. Pat yourself on the back for the head start. Make sure there's room to add more. Collecting and completing documents is more important than how they're stored.

Paper or digital? Both. Have a written or printed copy of the information and a digital version as well. Depending on preferences, you can handwrite or use the computer – just remember to update information and backup files regularly. Working digitally allows for easier updates and sharing. The Digital chapter has more information on this topic, but for now, just get started and keep it simple, accessible, and secure. Put files on a USB (thumb) or external hard drive and ensure that the people who need your information will have copies. Timing is everything. You don't know how much advance warning you'll get, so be packed and ready.

Keep in mind the most important thing: **papers point to people**.

It's not about the documents themselves, although they signal your intent and doctors and courts will recognize written instructions as legitimate. The most important thing is that these papers identify who will speak for you when you can't speak, your trusted people. Use the papers as a conversation starter, as a reminder of your desires, and as validation of how you're facing down fear. These forms will provide guidance for the people you've named. Make sure that those you've chosen are willing to do their part by honoring your wishes. Initiating uncomfortable conversations while healthy can ease the emotional vortex created by diagnosis, illness and debility.

Fix the Roof While the Sun Is Shining

We'd rather not think about death and dying. It's scary. We may be like a little kid who thinks: "If I close my eyes and can't see something, it can't see me." If I avoid saying the four-letter D word, DEAD might not happen. Magical thinking won't protect us and talking about something doesn't cause it to happen. We can stick our heads in the sand, but ultimately the thing we fear will come to pass. Reality wins over denial.

So, before you need them, gather your resources. Because it may be too late:
- When someone gets a terminal diagnosis, or
- Is intubated and in isolation because of COVID-19, or
- Has a head injury from a car crash and is unconscious.

By that point, the battle is already raging and not knowing what to do only makes a bad situation worse. In those circumstances, it's time to activate your plan. Expecting a miracle would be a wonderful outcome, but don't count on that as a strategy.

To update or not? A one-and-done plan is better than nothing.

But set-it-and-forget-it may not work if your circumstances change. It may be something monumental, like being widowed or divorced. Or, it could be seeing friends experiencing interventions you know you wouldn't want for yourself. A periodic check-up can be useful to ease your mind by making sure your plan still matches your preferences, outlines your wishes, and includes a current list of your assets. Good enough is okay. We do the best we can. And, no matter how well prepared we are, there will still be hiccups. That's life.

Being Prepared: Practical Steps For Your Labor of Love

A typical pregnancy lasts 40 weeks, divided into stages called trimesters. As the end of pregnancy approaches, specific signs indicate that labor is about to start and the baby will soon be born.

At the terminal end of life, the process of birth-in-reverse leads to the soul's release from the body. Unlike birthing a baby, the timing is more variable, with a duration that could range from minutes to decades. Without a simple pee-on-stick test to indicate that time is near, most people choose to ignore signs and symptoms. And, with a sudden death, sometimes there aren't any indications beforehand. The beginning of the end often reveals itself only in hindsight. Unlike pregnancy with an abundance of reassuring resources, mortality is often wreathed in superstition and fear. We need a path that supports and sets survivors up for healing. Having gotten this far into *Good Goodbyes* means you're interested in preparing for your labor of love. No matter if you know you have only a few weeks to go or want to be ready for whatever life throws your way, your preparation will make it easier for your loved ones.

Disclaimer: Guidance in the Prepare section is for informational purposes only. Use the contents for guidance, but not for financial, legal, or medical advice. Discern your values, make decisions, and prepare documents, but consult a professional to ensure that the documents will do what you want them to do. You can't come back from the dead to fix mistakes.

Get Your Act Together Using These Prepare Chapters

Medical: The beginning of the end will start with a health calamity. An injury, accident, or illness will be your admission ticket to the fun house. Don't wait for an emergency. All adults 18 and older need advance directives that identify a proxy decision maker and give guidance for medical treatment. Consider this your statement of intent of what medical care you want in whatever circumstances. Be ready to go, because you never know…

Legal: You may think you don't own enough to make a Will worthwhile. But this document identifies two important people: your executor who will be your post-mortem personal administrator; and a guardian, if you have children. If you don't make a decision, the state will decide. You may not be happy with the law's choice and it will be too late to do anything about it. To make things easier on your children or simpler for those who will inherit, make a Will. Clear the heir-way.

Wealth: You worked hard for your money. You know you can't take it with you. But you can make it really complicated and painful for ones you love and leave. You may not live forever, but your debts may survive your death, at which time they become someone else's problem.

Stuff: Clean as you go, instead of leaving a mess that will become someone else's responsibility. Lighten up while you have the energy. Are there certain things that you want to go to special people? Anticipate a tumultuous time, and ease the way. Less is more.

Transition: When a doctor says that an illness is terminal, you are entering the threshold of the last phase of life. As your time on earth winds down, certain decisions need to be made. When do you say enough already? How long should you continue invasive treatments? Is hospice an option? Do you want to be an organ donor? Living on our own terms includes considering dying and deciding what you want.

Disposition of remains: I'm dead, now what? If you haven't made it clear or planned it by this time, it's out of your hands. Which may have been your goal all along. Someone else has to make decisions – fast. A dead body must be dealt with immediately. Death accessories and resting places can get expensive quickly. Fundraising for funerals is not fun.

Digital: Your body may not live forever, but the internet can ensure an eternal digital presence. Social media accounts are virtually immortal. Your digital legacy also includes granting access to bank and household accounts. Don't subject a loved one to having to get a court order for access to financial accounts.

Conclusion: The Promise of Preparedness

Take time to personalize the packing list based on your values and circumstances. Pack your "go bag" and have it ready for the journey. Planning and preparation can go a long way to calming chaos and relieving the anguish that accompanies a medical emergency. Ensure your wishes are clear and documents are easy to understand and find. You can't control whether the end will be a slow slide or an abrupt drop. But having your gear ready and a plan in place allows a measured response, not a panicked reaction, when you encounter trouble.

If it feels confusing, complicated, and scary as you anticipate doing this work, imagine how much more it will be for someone who's in the dark, without a light or a map, and trying to make decisions without your input. When it seems too much, remember who you're doing it for. Papers and preparation point to people. The documents are ABOUT you but FOR others. Love is a decision. Caring is the bottom line.

When it comes to end of life, hope for the best—but plan for reality. And take the blinders off as you head into the future to meet a known challenge. Welcome any miracles that come your way. Your moment awaits. Be a hero – act with courage and compassion. And when it's time, leave behind your very best. The promise of being prepared will make the most of your (mortal) life.

FIVE

MEDICAL

∞

THE END STARTS HERE

uring my time as a chaplain at Tampa General Hospital in Florida, Terri Schiavo resided in a hospice across the bay in Pinellas County. At age 26, Ms. Schiavo had experienced a cardiac and respiratory calamity that deprived her brain of oxygen, resulting in impaired consciousness and leading to a diagnosis of persistent vegetative state (PVS). PVS patients may be able to move and open their eyes, but they lack awareness. Normally, the public doesn't know about these trapped souls. But this woman's life became a matter of public record as her husband and parents fought desperately over how best to care for her.

And why? Because Ms. Schiavo left no instructions. She didn't write down her health care wishes. One woman's tube feeding became a political and religious hot potato over the meaning of life. The Florida governor, U.S. Congress, and even the President of the United States got involved. Ultimately, the husband's understanding of his wife's wish to not be kept alive on machines was upheld. Ms. Schiavo's marker bears witness to the fight. Instead of just the usual two dates of beginning and end, hers lists three years: 1963 - 1990 - 2005—representing her birth, when she "Departed this earth," and finally "At peace." Her grave also bears this epitaph: "I kept my promise." Ms. Schiavo's dying lasted 15 years, involved multiple court cases, and broke her family.

We tend to think of alive or dead as an on/off switch, but it's not that simple. Living/dying exists on a continuum—it's really more like a dial. An individual might lack awareness, but advances in medical technology and drugs mean that a body can be maintained for a long time. Doctors and courts have had to develop specific criteria and tests for identifying when someone is actually dead. Across the United States, care facilities maintain an estimated 25,000 to 40,000 sleeping beauties who exist in a state of permanent suspended animation.[47] Sometimes, they were incapacitated as children and too young to have had a voice. More often, these adults failed to document their medical wishes in advance. Their lives involve a tug-of-war between various stakeholders who claim to know best. We can hope these individuals with minimal consciousness are not tormented by their sustained imprisonment.

I never met Terri Schiavo in person. But I was privy to her medical secrets. During a professional development session, a member of the hospital's ethics committee projected a scan of her liquified brain, placed beside a normal brain for comparison. Whatever point the doctor was making is gone, but I took note: Ms. Schiavo's story strengthened my resolve to evangelize about the need for advance planning and having Living Wills prepared and available.

Trauma calls reveal how innocently the end can start—ordinary activities—where a moment of inattention meets human vulnerability. A two-year-old eats a mouthful of peanuts that clogs his windpipe. A curious toddler wanders into an unsecured pool. An unhelmeted teenager is thrown from an all-terrain vehicle. A kindergartner waiting for the school bus hit by a driver turning the corner. A teenager runs off the road into the water and doesn't escape. A family asks doctors to "do everything," not realizing that *everything* can look a lot like torture.

Everyone eventually encounters a health mishap. Medical care can result in a recovery, but occasionally the person has embarked on a journey of no return. Especially with younger people, a strong body and vulnerable brain can mean a changed life forever, and not just for the injured person. The whole family is traumatized. Some of the saddest exchanges with families were hearing their hopes for a miracle. With enough prayer, they believed their loved one would survive this particular catastrophe. It wasn't my place to mention that survival isn't enough and a miracle doesn't need the medical paraphernalia that swaddled their loved one. Sometimes the miracle is death rather than limbo without end.

Advance Directives (AD): Don't Leave Home Without Them

If you think about dying at all, you probably expect you'll die quickly. Here today; gone tomorrow. If that's your belief, go back and check out the Aware section of *Good Goodbyes*. The reality is that the older you are, the more likely (over 90%) you'll experience prolonged decline rather than a sudden death.[48] Keep that statistic in mind as you read this Prepare section. The end may be a long time coming. You probably won't gain Terri Schiavo-level notoriety, but her fame might not be something you want anyway.

A medical misfortune will launch the beginning of the end. If you're seriously ill, incapacitated, or unable to communicate, you need to have thought about that in advance. Under the ethical principle of substituted judgment, doctors and family members aim to make the decisions that the patient would have made if he or she were able to speak and decide. If no document is prepared or can be found, the state will identify who is authorized to make decisions.

What do you envision for yourself? You actually have some control, but having agency over ending takes planning. And one way to do that is with autonomy-extender documents. Every adult needs an Advance Directive (AD—also called a Living Will). This essential document has two parts – who and what. Who would you want making decisions on your behalf in the event of a medical emergency? What would you want done or not done? The advance care planning process assumes familiarity with common treatment options. You discern based on your values and how you'd like to spend your final days. Given the likelihood of needing medical care, an AD goes into effect sooner than any other estate planning document, but *only* if a patient cannot make healthcare decisions or speak for himself/herself due to unconsciousness or mental incompetency. It's not just about the medical interventions you think you'd want if you couldn't voice your preferences, but also about probable prognosis. Will you return to activities from your previous life? What level of existence would you be happy with?

Everyone has a different interpretation of what is appropriate treatment, often a reflection of religious beliefs. Members of the Jehovah's Witness denomination won't accept blood product transfusions, which can be challenging during surgery. Some religions object to amputations, organ donation, or autopsy. Honor your religious tradition. Personalize to your preferences.

Don't wait; anticipate. The best time to prepare these documents is before needing them. Use your AD as a conversation starter to talk about what's important. You don't have to make all the mistakes yourself. Thinking about another family's experiences may make you realize, "No. I don't want to put my family through that." Plan now so your wishes are honored later. To save yourself and your loved ones pain, you need to talk about what you would and wouldn't want – before a crisis.

Quality or quantity? If you're not sure, visit a nursing home, at least virtually. In long-term care facilities, patients may be languishing—immobilized, restrained, or unresponsive. Poke your head into patient rooms. The most impaired are not the lucky ones seated in wheelchairs in the hallway. Imagine yourself in that bed or wheelchair and decide if that future possibility is one you would want for yourself. Would you be willing to trade places with one of the residents? Use this visit as a wake-up call. Deciding what you don't want may be easier than figuring out what you want. A lack of forethought, fantasies perpetuated by media, or doctors' communication failures leave many with misconceptions about what medical interventions can accomplish.

What's your line in the sand? Discerning what you consider *living* or fullness of life can establish levels of impairment, pain, and dependency you find acceptable. For me, connecting with people, reading, and walking are important. At this point, if I temporarily needed to be intubated because of general anesthesia, I'd give consent. But based on what's important to me, I wouldn't want to be tethered to a tube, paralyzed with drugs, and unaware. To me, that's not living.

Although better than having no document, Advance Directives are not without problems. Even if you have an AD, is it retrievable? How will you make sure it's available when needed? If you've completed directives, ensure they're accessible in the immediate aftermath of an accident or hospital admission. If a form is locked up for safe-keeping, it can't provide guidance when urgent decisions need to be made. Some documents are vaguely worded or a patient's situation doesn't match specifics indicated on the form. A proxy may not even realize that s/he was identified as the surrogate decision-maker. Or a family member may choose to ignore the patient's stated wishes. When disagreement arises, physicians may defer to the wishes of a potential litigant, who is usually not the unconscious patient. Telling someone your desires doesn't take the place of a document. Verbal rather than written expression does not meet *clear and compelling* evidence guidelines. Writing it down may not make it happen, but *not* writing can lead to cases like those of Ms. Schiavo, whose fate rested in the hands of the legal system.

Fear can be a deterrent. Considering the possibilities and completing this form forces a confrontation with vulnerability and mortality. Also, the future-oriented timing is nebulous. "How do I know what treatments I'll want five or ten or twenty years from now? I can't even figure out what I want for dinner next Tuesday." This is not one and done. The choices you would make at age 25 are probably different than those you will make at 75.

The people who need copies of your Advance Directives are your primary care doctor, your healthcare proxy, and your next of kin. Use the document to initiate conversations about your specific desires. If you change your mind, update the document and provide the most recent version to those individuals. You can create and store a digital copy of your advance care plan. For example, the Virginia registry links your uploaded directives with your driver's license. The problem is that so few people have utilized that option, that caregivers don't think to ask about its availability or know how to access the system.

Reframe

In life-or-death situations, patients with no medical expertise, facing tight deadlines, and feeling ill and shocked are expected to fully grasp the nuances and implications of a highly complex, volatile situation. Even in the best of times, it's tricky to weigh risks and benefits, probabilities and potential outcomes, let alone while under emotional duress. Advance planning documents anticipate and assess potential clinical benefits, burdens, and risks under the guise of giving patients informed consent.

Informed consent asks patients to decide on the means, rather than the ends. How knowledgeable is a typical person about medical treatment options? How can someone without a medical degree determine what's appropriate? Doesn't it depend? Absolutely ask your doctor for his/her recommendations based on professional judgment: in what circumstances is intubation warranted? Dialysis? Tube feeding? Should an infection be treated with antibiotics? But remember that even physicians with their extensive education and training aren't always sure what would be the best treatment for themselves or their family members.[49] That's why it's important for each person to be clear about what makes life worth living and communicate that to doctors and family members. What is acceptable to you?[50] Are you okay with being bedbound and unresponsive? For how long would you willing to live like that? What you need to contemplate and explain is what is important to you. What matters most? What are my beliefs and values? In what circumstances would I not want to endure certain procedures or side effects? Your answers need to be part of your legal Living Will. Ensure that the care you receive is by invitation, not invasion.

And one more thing: instead of thinking about the hassle of preparing documents, flip the perspective. It's not just about you. Your preparation is an act of love that can spare your loved ones from the unfortunate and uncomfortable position of having to make decisions for you.

First Things First: Carry an ICE (In Case of Emergency) card

Thumb through your wallet or purse. What if you slipped on the ice, hit your head, and couldn't talk? A bystander calls 911 and EMTs show up. You probably have plenty of cards that identify who you are. Okay, but you're not talking. Who should the medics call? Have you set up a screen on your phone with emergency contact information? Can someone access your phone log to see the last person you've called? Do you have an emergency card? An ICE card contains information first responders need to start treatment, including:

- Medical conditions (e.g., heart disease, diabetes, high BP, low hemoglobin, etc.)
- Prescription & over-the-counter meds (name, dose, frequency).
- Tetanus: date of last shot
- Allergies
- Medical history: Surgeries & dates, conditions, implanted devices, blood type
- Very Important People (VIPs): Contact info for Next of Kin (NOK) or health care proxy
- How / where to access your Advance Directive (AD)

An ICE card has another benefit. If you're hospitalized and you keep getting asked the same questions about preexisting conditions or medicines you take, just hand the interviewer your ICE card. Make it easy for all involved. You can obtain an ICE card online or make your own.

Proxy: Who Will Play God For You?

We often don't think about life's big questions, until we're immersed. One issue raised by the Schiavo situation: who is authorized to make medical decisions? And a question that gets to the root of our belief systems: what is morally correct in certain circumstances? These biggies: Whose right? Which person's right takes precedence when there's disagreement? And, who's right? What is the ethical response when the response or path forward is not clear? Thorny existential ponderings like *what's life*? And what's *alive*? These are hard enough to wrap your head around while drinking wine around a fire. But when you're asking them about a loved one on *life* support, they become high stakes. A patient who hasn't made her wishes clear complicates things, which may then become agenda items for ethics committees or courts, playing out in the media. Is that how you want your 15 minutes of fame?

People criticize the idea of other humans "playing God," but we've already adopted God proxies, whether we've entrusted health care professionals or judges. If you haven't expressed an opinion, someone else has to. Who will be your almighty? Will you place your faith in doctors, some of whom you may never have met? Will you accept whoever state law designates? Or will you just take your chances, figuring you're impaired anyway and having lost your ability to render an opinion, it no longer matters? If you want some control over your medical care, you have to think, decide, and do.

- Think – Consider the stage you're at in life and the treatments you might want.
- Decide – Choose a proxy and express your preferences.
- Do – Write down your wishes. Talk to your chosen surrogate.

When choosing your decision-maker, go for bonds over blood. Choose a proxy decision maker who shares your values and is willing to ensure that *your* wishes are followed. And do it before you're in an ambulance or in pre-op awaiting surgery.

Specialty Advance Directives

Five Wishes[51] is an enhanced advance directive. When completed and signed, the first two wishes meet legal requirements for an Advance Directive in 44 states and the District of Columbia.[52] Wish 1 identifies your health care decision maker[53]: who you want making care decisions when you can't. Wish 2 covers the kinds of medical treatments you'd want, or not. The other three Wishes address matters of comfort, spirituality, and final wishes. For example, Wish 3 asks you to think about pain management and hospice care. The 4th Wish asks if you want to be at home and if you'd like pastoral support. The 5th Wish covers final messages and preferences for body disposition or memorial events.

Just in case your head's not already spinning, there's another twist: a dementia Living Will. If you or someone you love has a family history of dementia, this form provides a codicil to the regular AD with specifics for anticipated irreversible cognitive incapacity. Courts sometimes raise a catch-22 with dementia cases, ruling that the current individual is not the same person who initiated and signed the original document. If you had dementia, such as Alzheimer's disease, how much medical care would you want? A Living Will can ensure that you get the care you want and provide guidance to help loved ones with difficult decisions. Consider what you'd want, prepare the form, and share your wishes with your family. Do it now – because you never know…

For your consideration:

Advance directives are *legal* documents, but you *don't* need a lawyer to prepare them. Download the form for your state or purchase Five Wishes, if it's valid for your state. You must sign your documents in the presence of adult witnesses and/or a notary public, verifying treatment wishes and ensuring you're of legal age and sound mind. Your health care agent should *not* be one of the witnesses. Different states have specific rules, which may be enough of a reason to have a lawyer prepare this form as part of your estate plan.

Given the choice, most people would choose divine intervention over advance planning. Although, in our modern era, we tend to look to science rather than religion for our miracles. Some families expect Lazarus instead of Rip Van Winkle. Many patients and families are inclined to embrace magical thinking, ranging from the expectation for a miracle (which by definition doesn't require a hospital or health care) to optimistic misconceptions about what *heroic* procedures entail and can accomplish. My chaplaincy supervisor, Wayne, suggested affirming families who awaited their ICU phenomenon with the phrase: "Wouldn't that be wonderful!"

Finally, your advance directives will remain in effect unless you revoke the authority granted by the documents. If you change your mind, you can recover copies you've handed out or replace an outdated version with a newer one. Or you die, and the need goes away…

Hearsay Won't Hold Up

If you're unable to advocate for yourself and haven't completed advance planning, you leave yourself open to the beliefs, whims, or guilt of others. Someone who objects can get courts involved, which will take time and money, prolonging the agony and adding complexity. If you don't have your wishes written down or the documents can't be found, your desires for medical treatment or its refusal are considered hearsay. You want a written record. But also make sure you have conversations that clarify.

Conclusion

Terri Schiavo is the spirit guide for *Good Goodbyes*. Her story has resonated with me beyond the time I spent in Tampa. During a recent visit to Tampa Bay, my chaplain friend, Susan, and I made a pilgrimage to the cemetery where Ms. Schiavo's remains were interred. The visitor's center refused to reveal the location of Terri's grave. Even after many years, she appears to still be the subject of controversy and not resting in peace.

Keeping her situation in mind, if you do just one thing, have your medical directives in order. Advance medical planning is essential for any mentally competent adult. An Advance Directive document will help maintain your autonomy, identify your intent, and mitigate disagreements. As with each Prepare chapter, use your values as a touchstone: What's important? Who's important? What makes life worth living? Make decisions after checking your principles.

Health care is designed as a bridge that can provide support while returning from the land of injury or illness back to fullness of life.

But we need to remember that the human body has built-in obsolescence. Being medically prepared gets you thinking about what makes life worth living. How much pain and how many procedures are you willing to tolerate? How much do you lose or remove before you're no longer you?

End of life is more than making intellectual decisions about your body. Also, consider the emotional impact on your loved ones. Show you care for those who may be called on to make decisions on your behalf. Put your love into action.

Reflections:

- What matters most to me?
- What do I consider a good life? What would have to happen to have it stop being good?
- What do I want for the people I love? Is my failing to plan protecting me or my family?
- Will whomever I've entrusted to speak on my behalf be willing to abide by my wishes rather than impose their own values or desires?

Actions:

- ICE card easy fix: Grab a business card from your next of kin (NOK), write ICE on it, and carry it in your purse or wallet. At least, your loved one will be alerted in case of emergency.
- Slip a business card between your mobile phone and its cover to have a better chance of recovering your device if it's lost.

Resources:

- Advance Directives by state: https://www.aarp.org/caregiving/financial-legal/free-printable-advance-directives/
- Five Wishes Advance Directive: https://fivewishes.org/five-wishes/individuals-families/individuals-and-families
- Dementia Advance Directive: https://compassionandchoices.org/end-of-life-planning/plan/dementia-provision/
- Storing your Advance Directive: https://www.nhpco.org/patients-and-caregivers/advance-care-planning/advance-directives/storing-your-advance-directive/

SIX:

LEGAL

∞

CLEAR THE HEIR-WAY

"I might be able to think outside the box, but when the box is six feet under, I'm not so sure." ~Warren Buffett

If there's a worst-case scenario, it happened to my neighbors. At a nearby house, a young mother was stabbed and killed just days before finalizing a contentious divorce. Bonnie was separated from her husband and had filed a protective order against her soon-to-be ex. On an April morning, a neighbor had seen the children, then ages 3 and 5, wandering alone outside in their pajamas. When police investigated, their mother's body was discovered. Due to a lack of physical evidence, no suspect was identified initially. It took six months before the estranged husband was arrested and charged. Eventually, he was tried and convicted of first-degree murder, a guilty verdict carrying two life sentences. Neighbors were relieved, knowing that this killing wasn't random, but there was no joy in justice—the kids witnessed a brutal murder; they lost both parents; a family was destroyed.

Were the woman's affairs in order? Only she and her family know, but it's possible she was waiting for the divorce to be finalized before completing new estate documents. Given the complexities of this situation, it may not have made much difference, since the criminal trial and appeals dragged on for years. Bonnie's family stepped in to raise the children and dispose of assets. A bad outcome could have been even worse if there had been no relatives willing and able to adopt the children.

Take heart. Whatever small steps you take, your family will likely be better off than what happened with my neighbor.

Planning Procrastination

Murder is an act of commission, an intentional crime of violence and hatred. Failing to protect loved ones is an act of omission. It may be unintentional, whether for reasons of fear, inertia, or not knowing better.

The idea of death triggers instincts for self-preservation: "If I ignore reality, I can pretend dying is not ahead." Not planning can mean inadvertently inflicting pain. And after the shock and sadness wear off, your survivors may wonder whether your failure to plan was a sign of not caring. Don't leave your loved ones with doubts; your actions speak louder than words. Act on your love. Plan for tomorrow, today.

The idea of "estate" planning is burdened with baggage. It seems unpalatable – an admission of mortality, which makes the topic unpleasant, difficult, and easy to avoid. Instead, think of it as a love letter or refer to it as legacy planning. Legacy is future-oriented; planning for tomorrow, today. Look beyond your current fears. Put yourself in someone else's shoes and imagine yourself easing their burdens at a bad time.

Some Common Justifications For Planning Procrastination Include:

Excuse 1: Too small. "I owe more than I own. It's not worth the trouble." It's about more than money. Do you have minor children? Who will be their guardian? Do you have a body? Every adult needs a plan for future health care needs and possible incapacity. Before death, everyone will be debilitated, whether for a short while or a long stretch. Who do you want making decisions on your behalf?

Excuse 2: Too many unknowns. "We can't decide who we'd want watching the children. Or what treatments I might want for whatever injuries or illnesses." It's so inconceivable and nebulous, like trying to decide what you might want to eat or where you might vacation next year. Make good-enough decisions with the information you currently have. Don't expect the process to be one-and-done. You can modify as needed – as you get older, as your health status changes, as your children reach maturity, or if you move to a different state.

Excuse 3: Too expensive. "I can't afford it." That thinking may be penny-wise and pound-foolish. Not planning ahead will take longer and cost more for your survivors than if you had done it while you're alive. Deferring to the future saddles your loved ones with expenses, like inviting someone to a meal at a restaurant and sticking them with the bill. Your investment now will pay off later.

No plan, possibly big problems. Your planning is protection. Without documents, the possibility for conflict grows. Like life insurance that pays out upon death, the rewards of estate planning are post-mortem. The main intangible benefit is love. In life, we try to safeguard the ones we love. Protecting our families continues after we are gone by providing clarity, reducing their stress, saving time and taxes, and ensuring simplicity and privacy. Having something is better than waiting for the perfect time or a perfect plan. Life changes and we face new circumstances. Just like clothes worn as a teenager won't fit a middle-aged body, your estate plan will also need to adapt.

Disclaimer:

I am not a lawyer. *Good Goodbyes* is not a legal document but is intended to provide general information, and to motivate and empower. Have an attorney draft your documents or at least review them to ensure their validity and confirm that they'll hold up to scrutiny. If problems arise after you're declared incompetent or dead, it's too late.

Where There's A Will, There's A Way

A physician tries to ensure your airway is open so you can breathe. An estate lawyer tries to clear the heir-way, so your survivors have a defined path during a tumultuous time.

Your legacy plan includes four fundamental documents. Two legal essentials are a last Will and testament (usually referred to as a Will) and a durable power of attorney. Two necessary documents related to health care are a medical directive and a proxy designation (See the Medical chapter).

Losing a loved one is not only an emotional journey. Your survivors will also have to settle your estate, an unsettling process that can be complicated, especially if information first has to be unearthed. You don't need much imagination to realize it will be a trying time. If your heirs have to undertake a scavenger hunt to find out what you've done or haven't done, the process can drag on for months or years, with no guarantee that everything will ever be found. The more that you decide and document ahead of time, the more the focus can be on what matters.

The purpose of a Will is to carry out the deceased's wishes (that will be you). What will happen to your estate after death? The Will tries to make sure your assets – any property or wealth – will pass smoothly to the intended people and causes and can provide your loved ones with peace of mind during a time of sadness and uncertainty. Without a Will, not only is there the possibility that you're putting your family at risk, but you have surrendered control as to how your property and estate will be divided. Without legal instruments, the law decides. Having a Will saves time and money. If a court has to step in to resolve issues, there may be delays distributing assets. Added to that are additional costs for a more complicated legal journey. And the cherry on top – added stress due to grief, ambiguity, and unfamiliar circumstances.

When my friend's former brother-in-law died, her niece and nephew were heart-broken. Their parents had divorced and their now-deceased father had remarried. When their father died without a Will – intestate – the laws of the state determined how his assets would be distributed. His estate passed to his current wife. The children from his first marriage were out of luck – disinherited. One might think their father would have known better—he was a medical doctor who had suffered two previous, nearly-fatal heart attacks. One might presume that he understood the risk that severe heart disease meant he could die suddenly at any time. Failing to make a Will, and avoiding the difficult conversation letting them know his reasoning, left his survivors hurt and disillusioned. Their father's failing to plan felt like a posthumous slap in the face for his children. They questioned his love and their impressions of a good relationship with their father, and death eliminated any chances for reconciliation.

Their story captures the grief caused by dying without a Will. Just like other things, not choosing is choosing. If a person hasn't prepared a Will, the state decides how your assets are dispersed, an option that will be more expensive, intrusive, and time-intensive. You may not be happy with the mandated distribution, but so what – you're not around to object. The ones most hurt will be the ones you claimed to love.

"Tag, You're It": Papers Point to People

A Power of Attorney (PoA) is a permission slip. It authorizes a trusted friend or family member to pay bills and make choices on your behalf regarding financial or legal matters, if you are unable to do so. During life and when needed, the person designated in your durable power of attorney can make decisions about everything *except* medical care. *Durable* means the document will remain in effect even if you become mentally incapacitated. You want to act while you're alive and competent, to extend autonomy even while debilitated. Just be aware – your durable PoA document expires when you die.

You're gone. Now what? Who will represent you? People may think that the sole purpose of a last Will and testament is to dispense property. The "what" is a partial answer. The Will also identifies "who" – your key people. Your Will designates your executor – the person who will settle your affairs. It also indicates who will raise your children, adopt your pets, and receive your treasure. When death terminates your

PoA's responsibilities, representation gets handed off to your executor. As your surrogate, the executor's role is to locate beneficiaries, collect and value property, distribute assets, notify creditors, pay debts, and file tax documents with the IRS. It's a complex job and not for the disorganized or faint of heart.

If you have minor children, your Will identifies guardians. Who do you want raising your offspring? If there's a surviving parent, he or she will take over. But you don't want your children suffering because you haven't prepared for contingencies, such as both parents being unable due to death or disability.

Will or trust: That is the Question

Do you need a trust or will a Will do? A trust is an optional legal instrument that facilitates getting property to intended recipients without going through probate. A big advantage is the possibility of simplicity, at least for your heirs. Not everyone needs a trust, but it has these benefits:

o   Provides control by extending autonomy
o   Saves time
o   Allows privacy

If you think you want a trust, you'll most likely need a lawyer, because there are multiple types of trusts, whether revocable or irrevocable. A revocable trust allows you as its creator to maintain control of assets while you're alive. The trust then directs how assets are distributed after death. Even if you have a trust, you'll want to have a pour-over Will to handle anything that's not included in the trust. Creation of the legal documents is only part of the work. You have to "fund" the trust by transferring ownership of assets to the trust by changing account registration. Your trust only controls the assets you put into it.

Probate

Probate is post-mortem, court-supervised distribution of belongings and payment of bills. When you die, your belongings (the legal term is *estate*) will go through probate. Probate takes place in the county or city of your last residence. It may be dull, painstaking, and expensive, but it's often mandatory if you owned real property (house or land) or had assets valued at over $50,000. In most states, a "small estate" does not require probate, so keep that $50,000 threshold in mind. Your assets add up. If you owned a car, the worth is based on Blue Book value. But, if you own property or a home OR have possessions and accounts worth more than $50K, your estate must go through probate court before assets are handed out.

A Will specifies who gets what, but some things pass automatically to heirs outside of probate, such as assets held in trust, life insurance and retirement accounts with named beneficiaries, or jointly held property. For example, your life insurance beneficiary is whomever you've designated to receive the death benefit when you die. You can cause lasting problems if you don't update beneficiaries. Even if you have indicated another person in your Will, by law, the named beneficiary will get the life insurance payout. If you're divorced and want a different beneficiary, change the designation on your accounts. Otherwise, the money may not go to your intended recipient. Unintentionally disinheriting a current spouse doesn't make for a positive lasting impression, although your former spouse may be delighted with the windfall. Don't screw this one up. You'll do your loved ones a disservice if you fail to make these changes.

Simplify. Make it easier on your beneficiaries by planning ahead. If you do it right, you'll ensure privacy about your estate (It won't matter to you. You're dead. What do you care?) and ease the way for your executor and heirs.

One more thing: if you own a business, develop a continuity plan to ensure for its orderly transition, a process called succession planning. Have a lawyer help you figure out the necessary steps. Your employees will thank you for being proactive.

Conclusion

Life is busy. The topic of *estate* planning, code word for *death* planning, is unpleasant. What needs to happen is not secret, but it is complicated. Death entails a point of no return and no fixing mistakes. But without someone pushing us to act, estate planning is easy to put on the back burner because it doesn't seem essential, until it suddenly becomes imperative and overwhelming. Our avoidance feeds anxiety.

Pass it on. Write a love letter. Who do you love? What do you love? Don't leave it to chance. Life happens, but there are certain things you can do. Prepare the legal documents that will identify who will raise your children and designate how your assets are distributed. Because once you're gone, it's too late to change things. How will your loved ones remember you? Even if you think you won't care how your heirs will view you since you'll be out of the picture, at least complete the four essential end-of-life documents: 1) your medical directive, 2) your health care power of attorney, 3) your Will, and 4) your durable power of attorney.

Failing to plan is planning to fail. While death may seem sudden, it's not unexpected. There's no time like the present to get your estate act together. Make a resolution to start. Now is the moment to invest some time to begin your estate plan or review an existing plan. Your survivors will thank you for caring enough to face your fears and for paying love forward by making it easier for them. A lawyer can help ensure that you leave no surprises and no disasters behind. Your legal documents will be a lasting "I love you."

In a note found by police at the crime scene, Bonnie was optimistic about the future: "I am determined to have a different ending to my story."[54] Her happy ending didn't happen. But realize: it's not so much the ending, every human dies. What matters are the penultimate and posthumous stories – what happens before and after the end – how we will be remembered. We can't change the fact that life ends in death. What we have some control over are things that happen before we get there.

If you're reading this, you have time to change the ending to your story. But like most people, we usually think we have all the time in the world. Until we don't…

Reflections:

- How can I make things easier for everyone?
- Does my executor understand the responsibilities that the job will entail (inventorying assets, closing accounts, distributing bequests)?
- Is my executor clear about my wishes and who gets what?

Actions:

- Tell your executor where your Will is located. After you die, nothing happens until the original Will is located. Filing the Will and death certificate initiate the process of probate.
- Defuse potential bombs by explaining your intent in a Letter of Instruction. File this document with the original copy of your Will.

Resources:

- Minimum essential: If you do just one thing, follow the steps in this state-specific planning guide https://eforms.com/estate-planning/

SEVEN:

STUFF

∞

LIGHTEN UP

"One of the reasons people get old – lose their aliveness – is that they get weighed down by all of their stuff." ~Richard Leider

"There isn't even room for a puppy to lie down." Kristine reported to us on the state of our friend's house. Patty had a neurological episode, similar to a stroke. When it became clear after hospitalization, surgery, and rehabilitation that she needed to move in with her family, women from our circle stepped in to clear out her home. Yikes! To our surprise and dismay, the house was jam-packed. Stuff was haphazardly stacked from floor to waist high, cabinet contents spilled onto counters, and even the bathtub overflowed. A mail-strewn path barely allowed access. A squad of friends pulled together to help clear her apartment and storage units.

There can be silver linings to unfortunate events. Helping our friend not only brought group members closer together, but it helped inspire this chapter. Patty's gift is to remind us we don't know what circumstances lie ahead.

Contrary to the bumper sticker message, "He who dies with the most toys wins,"[55] we seem to have forgotten that enough is good and too much becomes overwhelming. Being surrounded by your belongings may be comforting, but what happens when you're gone? Have you thought about who will have to clean up in your wake? The ease of online ordering and thrill of having a package arrive at your door can turn us from human beings to human consumers. Excess acquired becomes a nightmare delayed. We manage to keep it under control until something like a sudden debility reveals our dark secret. Ignored bills and junk mail become a deluge. Heaps of belongings have not only a physical weight but a psychic heft, including fear of exposing the mess and debt incurred by excessive spending.

Assess the Essence

Let there be light. A block of marble has a statue inside waiting for an artist to guide its birth. Chiseling stone, chipping away excess, and finessing until the core emerges. When Renaissance artist Michelangelo was asked about the statue of David, he explained: "I saw the angel in the marble and carved until I set him free." The sculptor discards purposefully, freeing the essence from a hunk of stone.

Likewise, the raw materials of possessions have an angel inside and are clues to our uniqueness. Who am I? Who would I like to be? The things we surround ourselves with provide a partial answer. It's our life-long endeavor to discern who we're meant to be and let that vision emerge. Our belongings are a physical manifestation of identity and aspirations. The seed is hidden; its flourishing awaits your tending.

Releasing material goods can be a spiritual and practical process. Clutter-clearing guru Marie Kondo sees the tidying process as both ritual and chore. With the reverence of approaching a shrine, Kondo enters a residence and takes a moment to address the house. She senses its center, kneels down, and bows. Our living space is our inner sanctum, the holy of holies. Becoming more intentional, curating what crosses the threshold, and deciding what things we hold onto becomes more than simply sorting, storing, and discarding.

Reframe clearing as nurturing. What do you ask of your surroundings? Are you looking for joy and tranquility or energy and creativity? Your answer might depend on a room's purpose. Like a miner who sorts gold nuggets from silt, decide what qualities you seek and filter out the remainder. Determine whether a particular possession or activity deserves a place in your life. The emotional weight of physical clutter can distract and block clarity of thought. Removing unnecessary items from your environment releases the psychic threads of inanimate objects that no longer serve. Your environment simultaneously reflects and affects your mindset. If you're looking for inner calm, aim for outer order. For a lighter or brighter demeanor, craft your space to mirror those same qualities. Remove excess so the essence can emerge. Live your truth by shedding dead weight and silencing the noise of too many things begging for attention.

Let Go. Pass It On.

"Have nothing in your houses that you do not know to be useful or believe to be beautiful."[56]

To keep or not to keep… Tidying your environment can be a proxy for clarifying your life's purpose. Committing to the discernment process is the first step. Imagine the life you want to live and what you need to get there.

What seems to be getting in the way or blocking the flow of energy? What thoughts, objects, or relationships feel toxic, draining, or heavy? Releasing can be painful. Stumbling blocks can trip you up. Clutter has a sunk cost. We've already spent time and money. Relinquishing can be emotionally taxing, leading to decision-paralysis. We delay because we can't decide. Psychic connections to an object, whether of a peak moment experienced or a love lost, can make discarding the symbol feel like abandoning a memory or person. Getting rid of something that's still "perfectly good" brings judgment—we threw away good money. And then there's not wanting to increase the earth's garbage burden. We hate to add to the waste, but finding a suitable home for our discards feels like complicated matchmaking.

Reasons to keep something include:

- Useful: Do I need it and use it?
- Beautiful: Does this make my heart sing? How many lovely items can I display or store?
- Sentimental: Does this remind me of a peak life experience?

How do you decide what makes something a keeper? Be aware: the bounty of beautiful and sentimental objects can easily get out of hand. There are many lovely things in the world. They won't all fit in your space. Focus on matter that matters. The same with physical objects with memories attached, the tangible reminders of intangible emotions – diplomas, yearbooks, or a flag that draped a loved one's casket. You need to find a balance that's right for you, but if keeping means having to rent a storage unit to handle the surplus, it may add to the burden instead of honoring the memories.

A Plan

If you are willing to take the time and are so inclined, go through your stuff slowly and methodically. Set up a schedule or a routine that allows you to mindfully sort, give away, or dispose. Take time to tend while you can.

- Visualize the end game. Picture how you want your space to look. What steps will make your image a reality?
- Imagine how a clearer setting might change the opportunities available.
- Plan your work; work your plan. Your house didn't get stuffed in a day. Think baby steps. Break up the large project into do-able chunks. Don't set yourself up for failure with an unrealistic timeline.
- Be discerning. Keep and display what you love.
- Enough, rather than more. Recognize limits. Knowing what's sufficient is a virtue.
- Simplify. Know when to add and when to take away.
- Embrace your preferences: if something works for you and the others you live with, that's what matters.

Sorting treasures from trash is simple but not easy. Letting go is like peeling an onion:

1. Start with yourself. What do you want and need? Keep what's useful, beautiful, or sentimental, but not too much.

2. Ask family and friends what they would like or want. Don't wait. Give it to them now so you can share in their enjoyment.
3. If things have monetary value, consider selling them. Cash is more liquid, and easier to maintain, than possessions.
4. Donate still usable things to charity.
5. Recycle or dump.

Sorting Questions

> "Anything you cannot relinquish when it has outlived its usefulness possesses you, and in this materialistic age a great many of us are possessed by our possessions." [57]

If only house clearing were as easy as the house selection process in the *Harry Potter* books, in which an enchanted hat decides where wizards-in-training belong. If your magic wand is misplaced ("I know it's here somewhere"), ask for a friend's help as you go through this process.

Set rules for sorting and discarding. What gets pitched and what do you keep? My personal sticking point is the rationale: "Just in case… It might come in handy someday." Maybe it will, but only if you can find it when you need it. Duplicates will multiply when we need something, can't find it, and acquire another.

Would you buy it again now? How much of a professional wardrobe do I need if I'm working from home? Will fewer outfits suffice? Does this blouse still fit my style? Does that skirt still fit? Do I even wear skirts anymore?

Is it easily replaceable? You may decide to ditch the dishes, but *don't* dump vital documents. Make sure to keep birth and marriage certificates or deeds, even if you rarely refer to them.[58]

Here are some other magical questions to ease your keep-or-toss decisions. Choose a rule that works for you:

- Clutter Consultant Marie Kondo's signature question: "Does it spark joy?" Pick up or touch an item. Does it generate a thrill? If yes, keep it. If no, let it go.

- Kris Hanson considers: "Does this speak to my passions: who I am and what I love? I'll keep items that connect to a passion, a joy, or a truth about me, or about the riches of the time I have lived."

- Does it help me fulfill my purpose? Keep it if it inspires and resonates with your heart's truth. Otherwise, release it for someone else's benefit. In *First Things First,* Stephen Covey reminds: "It's easy to say 'no!' when there's a deeper 'yes!' burning inside."

- Put your space on an elimination diet. Stop bringing more in and whittle down what you have. Pare down to essence: What feeds my heart? What resonates with my soul? What needs to go?

It's all about flow. Maintenance is ongoing. Be aware of movement. You can't keep breathing in without exhaling. As long as calories in and calories burned are proportional, body weight is stable. If you balance the *in* and *out*, things will stay more or less the same.

Just remember: most things can be replaced, but we can never replace time we waste.

Consider Others—Your Trash, Someone's Treasure

Live with an eye to the end. We arrived with nothing and we'll leave the same way. Your life, your time, your money, your stuff. We leave it all behind. It's your choice. Sort, organize, and dump your stuff now. By starting the clearing process while you can, there's a better chance that your discard will become someone else's treasure. MK still feels delight about a rug she found "curb shopping" in her neighborhood. The bike that doesn't get used or the winter coat not needed may make life easier for another person.

Recognize what happens if you fail to prune your own possessions—your inaction means dumping on someone else who has to decide and act. When you're gone, your precious possessions become your survivors' burden to deal with and dispose of – hiring an auction house, renting a dumpster, or making excursions to donation sites. The hours/weeks/months after death will weigh heavy, not just from grief, but compounded by detritus.

Conclusion

Patty's illness and abrupt transition provided pearls of great price. The gift to her circle of friends included these lessons: life can change in an instant. Secret stashes and storage units eventually come to light. Even if you don't open an envelope, the bill doesn't go away. Excess may not bring happiness. Overload may implode. Maybe we don't need this much stuff...

What counts? Figure out what matters most and commit time, energy and resources to those people and purposes. Invest in experiences, so the memories become the souvenirs. As you become mindful of end of life, you may be drawn more to spiritual essence and less inclined to material collection.

The sculptor visualized David trapped inside the stone and helped release him. What is waiting to be born in your life? Expose the truth that sits at the core. As you move forward, focus on what you need and some of what you want, and be willing to let everything else go. Be grateful. Share the wealth. You can't take it with you. Less stuff and better prepared equals more joy.

Reflection:

- What excess needs to be removed so the essence can emerge?
- Does your space reflect who you are or who you want to be?
- What things would you grab in a fire, after making sure your loved ones were safe?
- Are you happy with how quickly you can find the things you need without significant searching?
- From the perspective of the people who will need to clear your home after you're gone, have you considered how easy or hard it will be for them?

Actions:

- Ask a friend (perhaps a realtor who "stages" houses for a living) with a discerning eye to walk through the house with you and get her opinion.
- Take a few hours to try on the clothing you own. Ask for a friend's help to develop a capsule wardrobe.
- Compile an operational manual for your house with information about capital improvements, renovations, and mechanicals. While you may take things for granted, it will be new to someone trying to figure out the repair people you use, the location of shut-off valves, or even the size filters the HVAC takes.
- Make a list of real and high value property you own or lease:

identify land or houses, including their location and deeds (or mortgages). Motor vehicles, boats, and airplanes: Where are they located? Where are the keys? Where do you store the titles?

- In a letter of instruction, list beneficiaries that you want to receive special belongings like jewelry, art, or collectibles. Unless you make specific designations in a Will or letter of instruction, you can't be sure the person will receive the intended item. Or, better yet, give items to people while you're still alive so you can have the satisfaction of seeing their reaction.

EIGHT:

TRANSITION

∞

ON OUR OWN TERMS

"Don't cry because it's over. Smile because it happened."[59]

People tend to shy away from death, which means being unprepared and then subjected to default medical protocols—brutal interventions in the name of "saving." Where are the role models? Who has plotted a path to a happier ending? My mother-in-law, Vera, was an exception. She faced the end her way. During her son's first semester in his Physical Therapy program, Vera visited his anatomy lab and watched the cadaver dissection for hours. Based on that experience, she decided to donate her body and initiated the paperwork.

Her children encouraged her to complete advance directives. A lawyer helped with the medical and legal documents, intended to guide loved ones and ease decision-making. As the years went on, medical maladies piled up: lung cancer metastasized to brain cancer; falls, hip fractures, dislocations, and replacements; multiple surgeries, chemotherapy, and radiation. The illnesses, treatments, and complications took their toll. Each time, Vera rebounded, but with less energy and stamina. After gallbladder surgery, she required high levels of oxygen. Scans revealed lungs that looked like broken glass. Her doctor suggested a ventilator. Upon hearing that she might need a machine to breathe, she was adamant: no tracheotomy or tube feedings. "I don't want any machines keeping me alive. When God is ready for me, I'll be ready too."

With her family's agreement, Vera's code status changed to "Do-not-resuscitate/intubate" (DNR/DNI). Her survivor's instincts prevailed; Vera's lungs cleared and her oxygen requirements decreased. Then brain cancer recurred. With increased pain and considerable headaches from tumors, she entered palliative/hospice care. Comfort was the goal.

On the day of her death, Vera was by herself when she fell and hit her head. The impact caused bleeding and swelling of the brain. She never regained consciousness. Because she was already under hospice care, she was not subjected to 911 protocols – no emergency room, intensive care unit, or intubation. Vera was able to stay at home, in her own bed. During her remaining hours, her family shared special moments and said their goodbyes. Having communicated her desires and having plans in place helped make her passing a time of grace and peace. A good goodbye doesn't eliminate the sadness that a life is ending. It just means that a person is realistic, practical, and clear about what matters most – easing the way for the people you love.

What about you? Who do you know who is clearsighted about the end and has prepared an intentional path? And if you don't know anyone, why is that? How are we so unprepared for something so utterly predictable?

My immediate family has had a variety of death experiences: relatively quick, extended decline, and unknown. But no examples of *good goodbyes*. When my mother died at age 57 after a five-day hospitalization, her death was unexpected with calamitous aftershocks. My 48-year-old brother went missing and it was almost a month before his body was identified. He was alongside a hiking trail, without identification. The unknown cause and mysterious circumstances still contribute to lingering distress. When my father died two months after my brother, it wasn't surprising, given that he was almost 90. Years of dementia had contributed to physical and cognitive decline. After my brother's funeral, my surviving brothers and I discussed our father's precarious situation; health episodes had led to frequent ER visits, hospitalizations, and rehab – a cycle that was disorienting for him and exhausting for us. We approached my father's physician and asked about eligibility for hospice. He was admitted and ended up dying faster than predicted. But the good thing about hospice: it allowed him to stay in a familiar place rather than face mandated, often futile resuscitation attempts for those who lack a do-not-resuscitate (DNR) order.

Last Call

The Hail Mary attempt has failed. Your doctor has just informed you that there are no more treatments for the disease you've been battling with everything in modern medicine's arsenal. Or maybe someone you love is spiraling downward. The writing is on the wall: medicine has no more tools or tricks left in the bag. The countdown timer has suddenly gone from ticking to blaring. Your doctor is somber and compassionate when she says, "It's time to get your affairs in order." You know that day comes for everyone, but now suddenly it's your turn and you're shocked. Time seems to slow down.

Now what?

We are all terminal, but terminally ill has a special legal and medical meaning. If you've been told that there are no more treatments for your disease, hospice may be the next best step for you. It ensures quality of life, when quantity of time is limited. Hospice takes a holistic approach to the end, focusing on caring and comfort rather than curing. Hospice workers specialize in relieving pain and easing suffering, providing emotional and spiritual support tailored to a patient's needs and wishes. Hospice staff offer guidance and protocols for a good death.

Maybe your doctor hasn't said anything, but you're wondering if you or someone you love is ready for hospice. It depends. Here's a question requiring bravery. Ask your doctor: "Would it be surprising if I died within the next year?" If the answer is "No" – that death is a strong possibility – then hospice is an appropriate option. Doctors and patients must agree that the illness is terminal and there are no more curative treatments. Many doctors seem reluctant to broach the idea of hospice, even when life expectancy is measured in days or weeks, leaving families to initiate a request for palliative care (relief of suffering without addressing the root cause) or referral to hospice. Because of hesitancy about raising this fraught subject, enrollment may be delayed, limiting access to the full gamut of resources. Some think that admission to hospice is an admission of failure – death wins. That mindset disregards death's role as a universal outcome no matter how many life "saving" interventions delay the inevitability.

Health insurance, including Medicare and Medicaid, usually covers hospice care, but a patient is eligible regardless of ability to pay. The tricky thing is knowing when it's time. Unlike a pregnancy test, there is no definitive test that signals dying. Terminally ill is a subjective call: a physician certifies that you have six months or less to live, a challenging calculation given uncertainties about prognosis, especially with non-cancer ailments. Hospice can be extended as long as a patient is eligible, which means continued decline. For instance, Terri Schiavo languished at Woodside Hospice in Florida for a number of years, while loved ones and politicians battled over her potential for recovery. Hospice care is usually given where you live, in your home or a facility, like a nursing home. Some locales have residential standalone hospice facilities that may have specific eligibility criteria.

Illness can deprive us of spiritual closure when end-of-life belongs to medical protocols, intensive care, or pretense that another procedure or drug regimen will save us – extending length without enhancing quality. More often than not, doctors can find one more possible therapy. When a friend was telling me about her brother-in-law's weeks long stay in an ICU, I asked whether doctors had suggested hospice. She said, "No." His doctors had said it was too soon and they wanted him to try one more drug. The patient died hours later.

The paradox of hospice is that sometimes patients improve after curative treatments are discontinued. If a patient no longer meets the six-month terminal criteria, it's possible to disenroll. Although hospice offers a comprehensive approach to the last stage of life, it tends to be underutilized or entered late in the game, so the patient and family can't take full advantage of hospice services. Here's something to consider: survivors of hospice patients will continue to be ministered to during the bereavement phase. How many hospital intensivists continue to provide support to grieving family members?

Elements of a Good Goodbye

What constitutes a "good" death is not a prescriptive formula but arises from an individual perspective. If you have gotten a diagnosis that your life is on final approach, you definitely want to make sure decision-makers know your preferences. Ideally, you've pondered and discussed this topic ahead of time. If you refuse to think about what you want or fail to choose, you've relinquished your autonomy and someone else will decide for you.

As life winds down and by taking time to prepare, you can set priorities based on your criteria for a good goodbye. A good death speaks to completion and wholeness, integrity and empowerment, rather than the dying of the physical body. Most people would want their pain eased, suffering reduced, and dignity ensured. But a terminal illness or death of a loved one is a family affair. Prioritize comfort and pain control, but also consider how your dying will affect your loved ones. They are the ones who bear witness, provide caretaking, and possibly suffer repercussions.

What Happens as Death Gets Closer

As it was in the beginning... Generally, a natural birth involves no drugs or surgery, although expectant parents realize that an emergency may interfere with their hopes and plans. Access to technology has altered the determination of death. In response, different religions have weighed in on their definition of a moral approach to dying.[60] The Roman Catholic Church believes life has inherent dignity and insists that human life be protected until natural death occurs, a "consistent ethic of life" philosophy. And therein lies a mismatch between expectations and reality. What does *natural* mean? Does letting nature take its course entail foregoing drugs or surgery? When the body signals "death ahead" and medicine tries to interfere with dying, is that natural? How many brutal or futile interventions are natural?

Will yours be a natural death? Just like some women may not want to be conscious for giving birth, certain people may want a terminally sedated approach to death. Individual experiences may vary, but the dying process has certain consistencies. As the end of life nears, a person may withdraw emotionally, sleep more, and decrease eating and drinking, perhaps a counterpart to pregnancy's nesting instinct. When a loved one doesn't want food, we may be inclined to force the issue. A friend shared her family's deliberations about inserting a feeding tube to override her mother's refusal to eat. Even when a person has a cognitive impairment and the mind no longer functions well, the body seems to know when the end is approaching and will reject sustenance. Since patients and prisoners can legally be force-fed, it's important to be clear about what you want.

How We Want to Die

Allowing natural death does not mean forsaking pain medicine or hospital admissions. It recognizes and mitigates physical symptoms of dying, while being aware and caring for the suffering that can arise from unmet psychological, emotional, or spiritual issues. Anticipation of pain can be profoundly distressing. A patient fears pain and hopes nurses will be responsive and available when it's time for the next pill or shot. Under-treatment of physical pain can threaten integrity of the self. Care providers and families have a responsibility to ensure a balance between over-medicated, prolonged dying and appropriate use of practices to repair sick and injured bodies. A life lived for noble purposes differs from an existence without awareness, but a person must choose the path they prefer while they still have capacity to decide and act.

Euthanasia derives from Greek origin (*eu* "well" + *Thanatos* "death") and means good death. Given the alternative, wouldn't most of us prefer an easy death? Unfortunately, the word *euthanasia* has been hijacked and has assumed an altered meaning. Physician-assisted death, also called Death with Dignity or Aid-In-Dying, allows a doctor to prescribe medications at the request of a suffering patient. A patient, who qualifies based on strict criteria, acquires a lethal dose, which s/he can opt to consume in order to hasten the inevitable end.[61] While pain relief and palliative care should be standards of care to treat end-of-life suffering, some patients gain comfort from feeling in control and having their autonomy honored, even if they ultimately decide against taking the drugs. As of 2022, eleven jurisdictions permit physician-assisted aid-in-dying (see https://compassionandchoices.org for the most up-to-date list). But while the law may make Aid-in-Dying legal, many doctors and pharmacies won't cooperate, so patients still have limited options for honoring self-determination.[62] Diane Rehm's book, *When My Time Comes*, discusses Aid-In-Dying. She quotes a doctor who likens making patients take their own lethal dose to having them perform self-surgery to ensure their consent: "We have your permission to take out your appendix... Here's a scalpel, please do it."[63]

And what about taking drugs? *Double effect* is about doing something good that may have a bad side effect. Taking narcotics is acceptable, as long as the purpose is pain relief, even if it might unintentionally accelerate death by depressing respiration. The U.S. Supreme Court has weighed in on the topic, ruling on the legality of double effect: "If the intention is the relief of suffering or to help breathing, even if it increases the possibility of hastening an inevitable death."[64] Many religions that forbid physician-assisted death nonetheless allow the double effect of narcotics; pain relief outweighs shortened life. Intent is everything.

Where We Want to Die

Consider the ending. Of course, given the choice many people would opt out of dying altogether, which is beyond the scope of *Good Goodbyes*. But if you want to beat the odds about where you die, it won't happen by chance: "80% of Americans would prefer to die at home, [but in reality] 60% of Americans die in acute care hospitals, 20% in nursing homes, and only 20% at home."[65] COVID may have changed these percentages, with an uptick in institutional dying. But the point is, there's a gap between the setting most would prefer and where death actually happens. At a certain point, more care or hospitalization is not necessarily better. Intensive care units are focused on keeping patients alive, employing all of the medical therapies and technical apparatus available. An ICU death or one with aggressive interventions will not only be hard on the patient but it's also traumatizing for loved ones. Deaths will certainly happen in ICUs, but it's often a lonely, isolating, and unconscious experience. Is death the worst thing? If you accept death as reality, not possibility, it results in making choices based on the understanding that time is finite. The preciousness of this limit may help to orient and clarify life's path.

What Matters

The longer we live, the closer we get to the decline and eventual cessation of the physical body. The body's decay and weakening generates an existential imperative, affecting our physical state but also an often-un-acknowledged spiritual ache, a number that can't be pointed at on a pain scale. It arises from issues with meaning, connection, and hope. What's life all about? Are my relationships in good order? Will I have courage in the face of death? Given the expected ending, how can we make it meaningful? Can we override the cultural taboo that defaults to denying/delaying/deferring death? If we anticipate, can we decide how we want to die? Isn't that what autonomy, agency, and informed consent are all about? No one will fault you for wanting to live out your days pain free, holding people close, and preparing to meet your maker.

Our lives are like an iceberg: we see the visible part floating on top of the water, without paying attention to the bulk below in the depths. Focusing on physiological vital signs as the only measure of life neglects the profound human essence. If you agree with St. Irenaeus of Lyon's (202 AD) claim that "The glory of God is the human being fully alive," then it follows that dying well starts with living well, which requires each of us to define fullness of life and discern our life's purpose. What brings meaning to life? Facing the end can arouse despair and depression or evoke profound spiritual awakening and recognition of connections.

When people think about what makes life worth living, the love shared with others is likely to top the list. After meeting physiological and safety needs, humans seek connection and love. The primal urge of forging and strengthening relationships contributes to a meaningful life. A meaningful life is about moments rather than metrics, and peak experiences rather than vital signs.

In *Man's Search for Meaning*, Holocaust survivor Viktor Frankl mused, "Man is not destroyed by suffering; he is destroyed by suffering without meaning." A pregnant woman endures labor pains. She understands: labor is finite; if the pain gets too bad, there's recourse; and a baby will arrive as a reward at the end of her effort. Her pain has meaning. Less so with dying, unless you believe in an afterlife, which is a matter of faith. Without context or guidance, there's worry, fear, and pain, with seeming darkness as the outcome. No one helps us to make sense of physical pain or emotional suffering, added to which the not knowing whether our ordeal will exceed our endurance.

Expectant mothers realize you don't wait for labor pains to learn breathing exercises or collect a layette. Likewise, there's work to be done before getting to the end. Learning about stages of dying and techniques for coping are essential life skills. Using the iceberg analogy, think about how much attention is paid to the tip – trying to cure the physical body – while healing of the whole may be neglected. Doctors and patients talk in terms of treatment protocols or drug therapies, without addressing essential, existential questions, like what life has meant. Death is momentous and universal. We know it's coming and yet ignore or deny it until we blunder into it. In his book *Being Mortal: Medicine and what Matters in the End,* Dr. Atul Gawande writes:

> Two-thirds of terminal cancer patients reported having had no discussion about their goals for end-of-life care, despite being, on average, just four months from death. But the third who did have discussions were far less likely to undergo CPR or be put on a vent or end up in an ICU. Most of them enrolled in hospice. They suffered less, were physically more capable, and were better able for a long period to interact with others. In addition, six months after these patients died, their family members were markedly less likely to experience persistent major depression.... People who had substantive discussions with their doctor about the end-of-life preferences were far more likely to die at peace and in control of their situation and to spare their family anguish.[66]

Whether those who are dying reconnect with or renew religious beliefs or seek new religious experiences, they are likely to engage in some form of spiritual searching.

A Spiritual Experience: Birthing the Soul

How does one face the unknown? Pregnant women assume that they'll receive information and exercises to face delivery and birth—what to expect. What are the stages of labor? What relaxation techniques might ease pain and anxiety? Knowledge and preparation empower. Having an understanding and coping skills set the stage for an easier and more positive experience. Feeling some control over what's going on and knowing what to expect can be reassuring. An intentional approach to the beginning of life is expected.

Fullness of life means different things to different people. For some, a life worth living may be planning and checking off bucket list adventures. Others may prioritize volunteer service, find great joy golfing with buddies, or playing with the grandkids. If we keep in mind mortality and ability, we realize that there's no time like the present to act on our goals. Some of us will age more gracefully than others, but the older a person gets, the greater the likelihood for debility and chronic illnesses. Living a fuller, more abundant life needs to be planned, including contingency plans. The way doesn't always unfold in the way we expect. Facing our deadline can inspire taking time to ensure that important relationships are renewed or restored. Words of healing can aid in emotional closure: *I forgive you; forgive me; I love you; thank you.*[67] With the isolation of hospitalizations during COVID, many people didn't get a chance to exchange last words or share a blessing. On what ended up being the morning of her death, a friend typed her last words:

"Love you all. Bye Bye." What a memory of grace for her children. People must consider their legacies while reasonably healthy, energetic, and alert. Knowing that we will die gives a sense of urgency to how we live. There's no time to waste. The key to a good death is living fully, which includes not only acknowledging human ephemerality but also entails broadening identity beyond the body.

When it's time for birthing into eternal life, efforts often focus on trying to reverse the process, like trying to patch an eggshell, when the bird is trying to emerge. Sometimes fixing is appropriate, but not always. Eventually, everyone reaches the dying times, and usually we face it without guidance, preparation, or information. The transition into death is a no-expert zone, with many medical practitioners emphasizing life extension and death prevention. Doctors, patients, and even theologians have no special proficiency in dying, making it a do-it-yourself proposition. Do physicians have a moral responsibility to "save" a life when the outcome will incur suffering and dependency? Pretending there's no outer limit to physical survival has ramifications beyond a patient's well-being. Patients fear prognosis, treatment, and what's next, but evasion or deceit from medical professionals and caregivers has a cascading negative effect on families, finances, and future.

Contemplation can help us cope with overwhelming emotions and situations. Mindfulness, breath work (like yoga or Lamaze techniques), or prayer can aid in connecting us to inner peace and bring hope in challenging situations. While ongoing discernment (like an examination of conscience) is appropriate at any time, pausing, auditing, and resetting your life can be especially important at inflection points like retirement. This process can probe whether you're living fully, whatever that means for you, or whether a course correction is called for.

Essential Steps at the Threshold

Trying to vanquish a mortal enemy may have been pulling you in a dozen different directions. That's over. The doctor has said that your time is limited. It's hard to wrap your head around it. How can this be? While you still feel reasonably good, life has suddenly gotten pretty simple. This time is all about you. Delegate must-do things to others. If you only want an ice cream cone for dinner, so what? If you're so inclined, forget flossing, flu shot, or dental exams. What's the point? Do more of what you love and things that bring you joy.

Be gentle with others. Your family may try to convince you to keep fighting. Your friends may avoid you because they're afraid of saying the wrong thing. Ask them to just come and be with you. Forgive.

If you have the privilege of accompanying someone else in the end-of-life journey, use their experiences to figure out what you might want for yourself. The dying of others before it's our time can be a rehearsal.

If you've taken steps suggested in *Good Goodbyes*, you've already taken care of many practical details: completing lists, documenting wishes, and ensuring they're accessible. The people you love will know where to find assets and passwords and keys. Good. Now you can focus on what matters most during the time remaining. Some aspects of the dying process will be out of our control, but here are these aspects to consider:

1. Transition to hospice care. Focus on comfort. Take advantage of the interdisciplinary services. If you want prayer from a chaplain or a visit from a volunteer, hospice can arrange it. If you need equipment like a hospital bed or commode, the organization

will help you obtain it. Instead of going to the doctor, a nurse or doctor will visit you. If you need medications or supplies, hospice will arrange for them to be delivered.

2. Do what you love. Be with those you love. Your departure will leave a gaping hole. Now's the time to say what needs to be said to help heal relationships and bring emotional closure. Say the magic words: thank you; I love you; forgive me; I forgive you; goodbye.

3. You call the shots. Fixing your body now takes a back seat. If pain is a significant issue, use hospice's expertise to help manage it. If you're hurting and need meds, take them. There's nothing to be gained by suffering; don't be a hero. Don't worry about addiction. Do consider the balance between keeping the pain at a tolerable level and being zoned out. Also, take other medicines to deal with the side effects of narcotics, like nausea or constipation.

4. Stages of labor. Your body is shutting down. Your levels of mobility, activity, and cognition are probably deteriorating. Depending on the cause of death, you may be proceeding from fully functioning to needing total care. You might have wounds that don't heal, a urinary tract infection, pneumonia, or sepsis. Your Living Will should have addressed whether or not you want the source of infections treated or let nature run its course while taking meds for comfort.

5. Medical emergencies. If you're enrolled in hospice and pain or breathing gets suddenly worse, call hospice. A medical provider will respond to the patient's symptoms and provide support for the caregiver. If 911 is called and paramedics show up, EMT

teams are mandated to attempt resuscitation and transfer the patient to the ER, unless a person has a valid do-not-resuscitate (DNR) order or rigor mortis has set in.

6. Be open to spirit. Take time to care for your soul. Whether you reconnect with or renew prior religious beliefs or seek new religious experiences, you may be inclined to engage in spiritual searching. You may be experiencing that the separation between the earthly realm and the divine is becoming permeable and translucent.

7. Explore generativity, the giving of ourselves to others. Pass on your wisdom. Promote the future wellbeing of others. Embark on creative pursuits like legacy writing or storytelling.

Passages

People honor milestones with ceremonies. Rites of passage can help ease transitions by providing structure for commemorating. Rituals help us comprehend what's happening, navigate new stages of development, and celebrate status changes. Events like giving birth, baptisms, birthdays, reaching puberty, bar mitzvahs, graduations, earning a driver's license, or getting married are about crossing a threshold and accepting new responsibilities. A rite can help us deal with and heal the confusion or grief associated with endings. Rituals help simplify the complex and bring order to chaos. When we encounter a transition point, a ritual can help us know what to do and how to be, supported by others' strength and reassured that we are not alone.

This is where religion might provide guidance, instructors, and processes to encourage intentional life review to elicit a sense of perspective and purpose. When we know that our lives have made a difference and contributed to the greater good, arriving at life's end will signal completion, not obliteration.

To prepare for a rite of passage, we must plan and invest time and resources to complete tasks that set the stage. Practical measures – acquiring knowledge, developing skills, mentally preparing – are only the beginning. We must also engage in psychic work to honor the spiritual nature of this transition. We emphasize rituals that are important to us – joyfully celebrating beginnings. Since endings do not receive the same recognition in our culture, rituals are lacking for leaving home, job loss, miscarriage, divorce, aging, or dying.

Many people view the end of life as a downer. But what if we approached end of life as an epic rite of passage? Attending to others as they are dying and attending funerals, accompanying and bearing witness to the final chapters of others' lives, gives some practice. These rehearsals (for us), provide an opportunity to figure out what we want, or not. And then, when it's our turn, what's important is clearer, such as saying "yes" to hospice or "no" to chest compressions. Preparing for death can be instructive and life affirming by looking back – by honoring old roles, celebrating accomplishments, and pondering lessons learned. Looking forward allows us to step consciously into the life ahead by facing fears and taking time to consider preferences. Having a plan and a process before being in the thick of a predictable change can help ease upheaval and shock. It will still be hard, but the payoff will be a sense of comfort, peace of mind, and easing the burden for others.

Acknowledging and celebrating thresholds can wake us up to living more consciously. Death awareness practices are even embedded in certain religions. Benedictines are urged to "keep death daily before your eyes."[68] Reflecting on death helps illuminate life. Death denial comes naturally. But blocking that awareness means we're not ready when our time comes. When medical procedures engulf the end times, that focus limits the possibility for a spiritual experience. And, what could be an awesome occasion becomes an "Ah s#!t" ordeal.

Conclusion: Death as True North

"Oh wow. Oh wow. Oh wow."[69]

I will never know what happened with my brother before he died. Had he gone for a run from his apartment five miles away? Did he forget to carry ID? What was going through his mind in the days, hours, and moments before he took his last breath? My not knowing about Jack can't change his dying. But this experience—how failing to address death's certainty creates immediate chaos, unfinished business, lingering upheaval, and regrets from stories forever lost and important details not shared—has been a catalyst for trying to make a difference going forward.

What do you think you'll want when the end is near? To have machines and medicine keeping you alive in a sterile facility? Or to be in the comfort of your own bed at home? Life's outcome is predictable; the way most of us die is a failure. We expect a long, healthy life, and we don't expect death. We may abuse our bodies and expect the medical system to fix us. We don't make our wishes known, failing to signal our intentions or to guide decision-making. We cede responsibility to others and let them guess and choose, based on their values and standards, complicating an already volatile and devastating situation. Averting our eyes, pretending otherwise, refusing to face reality or prepare, our recalcitrance forces the hand of others and sets the stage for complicated grief. A good goodbye requires your cooperation. When the time for curing has passed, there will always be time for healing and caring.

Being aware of impermanence and the possibility of incapacity can be pearls of great price. This knowledge counterbalances the sorrow that life is ending by giving time to heal relationships, act on dreams, risk more, and appreciate loveliness. As earthly time winds down, ask others to honor your priorities. Each of us will only get one chance to write the ending. This awareness can remind us to live life to the fullest. Don't wait; you don't know when the last will be the last.

> Life in its passing is a sacred thing,
> never to be repeated.
> Let not a day pass
> in which you do not honor life's mystery
> or behold its wonder in your heart.[70]

Reflections:

- Since the world is filled with people who have never died, who will teach you about dying?
- Who do you know who has faced the end on their "own terms"? What would that look like for you?
- How do you envision the ending?
- Is death the worst thing?
- Think about criteria for a good death (pain free, having choices over treatments, a sense of completion, dignity, relationships healed, spiritual engagement, etc.). What is most important to you?

Actions:

- If you're expecting an ending where you go to sleep and don't wake up, make sure you've done the work so your death doesn't become an overwhelmingly traumatic event for those who have to deal with it.
- Don't rely on a doctor to suggest hospice. You may have to take the initiative and ask. And if the first hospice says the patient doesn't meet its criteria, inquire at another. Different hospices have different admission standards.

NINE:

DISPOSITION

∞

I'M DEAD, NOW WHAT?

"The truth does not change according to our ability to stomach it."
~ Flannery O'Connor

When Anne talks with her husband about her death and its aftermath, his response is always the same: "What do you care? You'll be dead." He has a good point. But here's the counterargument: when we expire, the decisions don't disappear. In many ways, they intensify. With death, a family is multitasking, trying to cope with a catastrophe at the same time they're planning a complicated event with a short suspense. If you knew that you could ease their efforts, wouldn't you want to?

The timing and location of death may be unexpected, but everyone's eventual outcome is universal. So, go ahead. Pick out the flowers, decide who to invite, choose a menu, and write the obituary so all that your family needs to do is fill in the blanks. Instead of thinking, "They owe me. It's their turn to take care of me," decide about details and discuss ahead of time. Your forethought will bring relief for those struggling with aftershocks from your passing. Your advance preparation will pay forward a last act of kindness and generosity. You cared enough to leave a plan in place.

It's always easier to work from a crappy draft than a blank page. That's an approach to consider with planning—something is better than nothing and done is better than perfect. Gather your thoughts and develop a general outline. If something is particularly important to you, like asking for charitable donations instead of flowers, emphasize that. Don't wait. It's your party. Figure out now what you want done and tell someone. Also, write it down and add it to your collection of essential documents. Otherwise, failing to plan shifts the burden to someone else who tries to guess what you might have wanted.

Anne's husband is right. When you're dead, you don't get a say—you'll be the silent center of attention. But behind each dying or dead person is a hurting family. Emotional turbulence can compromise judgment, and there will be limited time and energy for researching *Consumer Reports* or checking out the Better Business Bureau. Do you really want to force your loved ones to fundraise for your funeral? In the midst of dark days, make sure the path is clear, well lit, and easy to navigate. As you do advance planning, keep this question in mind: "How can I make things simpler for everyone?" Here are some issues your family will be facing: What's the best way to memorialize a life? Are you interested in letting others use body parts or organs when they are no longer of use to you? What about the final disposition of remains? People may have strong preferences. You won't know other's desires unless you ask. Others won't know yours unless you tell. Don't ask, don't tell – can lead to hell.

Death On Your Doorstep

So, you're teetering on the threshold. Maybe you didn't think it would happen quite so soon or quite this way. Circumstances aren't always within our control. But whatever has happened, you are now beyond thoughts and feelings. Doctors have indicated you don't have much time. We think of death as a binary, with a clear boundary between alive or dead, but that's not always the case. For many people, it's less like an on-off switch than a dial with a spectrum of degrees. At a certain point, there will be no more resuscitating or rescuing.

In death, as life, if you plan ahead you get more control over decisions, like what happens to the body you no longer need. Thinking about a life ending may be hard and sad. But a death can make it easier for someone else to live. As you hover in this in-between unconscious state, discussions will be swirling around you. Decisions have to be made quickly. If you've been clear about preferences, doctors will take that into account. If your family chooses to disregard your wishes, you can come back and haunt them. Autopsy, donation, and disposition are some immediate decisions your family is forced to make.

Autopsy is a surgical postmortem dissection and examination that tries to determine the cause of death and evaluate the extent of disease or injury. Under certain conditions, an autopsy may be mandatory, for example, if a death raises a public health concern; for someone who dies outside of a hospital or hospice care; or if death results from injuries, like a car accident.

Donation Options:

> "Don't take your organs to heaven, heaven knows
> we need them here."[71]

Many are called; few are chosen. Choosing to be an organ donor can give someone else a new lease on life. Donating your body or its parts can be a final expression of love and concern for fellow human beings, *supported by many religions*. Articulating your wishes is a thoughtful gesture for your survivors. If they know what you want, it can add peace of mind and simplify decisions. Many religions consider organ, eye, and tissue donation as a final generous act of caring. Even if you have been clear about wanting someone else to use pieces that you no longer need, there are options and decisions. In my life, I've been concerned about living lightly, sustainability and recycling, attitudes I want to continue with as I approach the afterlife. Can someone else use my body or its parts when I no longer need them?

Organs and tissue for transplantation must be removed immediately after death. For anatomical study, the body must be intact. So, one decision is between whole body or organ/tissue transplantation. You can do one or the other, but not both. Also, medical schools will not accept a body that's been autopsied. So, next of kin must decide whether to permit an autopsy or donate the body.

Organ donation: Some people are leery about agreeing to donation, thinking that doctors won't try as hard to save them.[72] Not so. Your life always comes first. If you are taken to the hospital after an accident or incident, it is the medical team's number one priority to *save your life*. Your status as a donor is not even considered until every effort has been made. Only when doctors have determined that no drugs, therapies, or surgeries can bring you back and you are on the cusp of imminent death, is when a transplant team may approach your family. If the circumstances of your dying permit, doctors will talk with your next of kin about donation. Donation is based on medical criteria, not necessarily age or health. If you're registered as an organ, eye, or tissue donor, doctors will assess whether or what organs can be used. A medical screening considers donation potential, evaluating organs (heart, kidneys, lungs, or liver) or tissue (eyes, bones, etc.). Even if you've indicated a desire to be an organ donor[73] in your Living Will or on your driver's license, your family or physicians may not be privy to this information. Your family has the final say. Some may view donation as redemptive – something good coming out of something bad. Organ donation almost always involves a hospital death because of the need for quick surgical intervention.

Body donation: Some restrictions apply. For body donation, you need to initiate the process while you're alive – each medical school has different needs, criteria, and forms. Considerations for acceptance into a donation program include distance to the receiving medical school, body weight (because of storage limitations), the cause of death, and whether major surgeries were performed. A medical school will generally transport a body to its facility (varying from 50 – 150 miles). After the study is complete, a family can opt to have cremated remains returned to them or buried with those of other donors.

COVID concerns: Transplant professional societies recommend that individuals who tested positive for COVID-19 and died of the infection should not be considered for organ donation.

Disposition of Remains

Body care after death is not usually a do-it-yourself proposition, but some aspects don't require a professional undertaker. Pragmatically, disposition of a dead body has limited options—bury or burn—but on an order-of-magnitude more fraught than deciding on "paper or plastic" at the grocery checkout. Like melting ice cream, this issue is time-sensitive. Because of the need to move fast, knowing your loved one's preference simplifies decision-making. Buried or burned are the two major options. For some, the thought of confinement in a narrow box decaying underground is unnerving and claustrophobic. Victorians acted on the worry of potentially, unintentionally being buried alive by equipping coffins with bells that would ring above ground and alert the grounds keeper. Others may have a strong opposition to cremation, because of remembrance of the Holocaust or for religious reasons. But if you haven't prepared and shared the information ahead of time, your family may feel compelled to make a different choice out of love, grief, or guilt. We're not at our best when we're emotionally distraught.

People have little experience with this aspect of life and limited opportunities to become proficient at funeral methods. Being clear ahead of time will take one more decision off your survivors' plate. Some people worry about spending thousands of dollars for a container that will be buried or burned. Besides financial concerns, the handling of dead bodies has environmental drawbacks. If being environmentally friendly was important to someone while living, you may want to minimize negative impacts as you weigh the pros and cons of burial versus cremation. The cremation process is energy intensive and releases pollutants to the air. With traditional burials, concerns include space issues, embalming fluid toxicity, and non-sustainable materials used to build caskets. Some cemeteries now accept green burials, so a body is interred with minimal covering and without preserving chemicals to allow for natural decomposition.

When you're deciding for yourself, you can keep practicalities, such as costs, in mind. Cremation is generally more economical, especially if there will be a delay between death and burial. For example, many who qualify for interment at Arlington National Cemetery can face a six-month or longer wait before burial. Cold storage for a body can be an expensive proposition. You may want to consider which options are least harmful for the earth. Body disposition can have a lasting impact for generations to come.

Different faith traditions have different perspectives[74] on body disposition. Whether for yourself or someone you love, the priorities will be for a dignified, reverent, and memorable departure ceremony. Funeral homes will ensure respectful body preparation and handling. Some cultures and faith traditions see a viewing as an important part of the ritual. Even with cremation, a viewing can take place beforehand. If death occurs in a medical facility, the staff may allow a limited gathering before funeral home workers arrive. Cremation is becoming more widespread in the United States, but certain religions, such as Islam, forbid it and many Jews dislike it. Although cremation was banned by the Catholic Church until the 1960s, it's now acceptable. The Catholic Church prefers that cremation takes place after funeral Mass and that cremains are buried, rather than scattered or kept at home.

With burial, a body is placed in the ground or a crypt. Having a body cremated expands the options since cremains can be kept in an urn, scattered, buried in the ground, or placed in a columbarium. There are other more exotic options for those who fancy themselves early adopters of new trends, such as water cremation (called resomation or alkaline hydrolysis) or a mushroom burial suit for biodegradable body disposal.

Celebrating Life

"You always wonder about your funeral. How big? Who'll show up? In the end, it's meaningless. You realize, once you die, that a funeral is for everyone else, not you."[75]

At a certain age, we realize that when something dies, it's forever. That almost unfathomable insight is at the crux of what it means to be human. Often during the dying process, the focus is on treatment, leaving families scrambling to accomplish tasks related to disposing of the body, writing an obituary, and arranging a wake, funeral, memorial, and internment. Even when death is expected, many people resist facing this transition until immediacy forces action.

The death of a loved one can feel overwhelming and exhausting, especially with having to attend to the details in the midst of grief. End-of-life rites, such as funerals or memorial services, focus on survivors. The commemorations help family celebrate the deceased and start adjusting to post-mortem life. This ritual occurs when the guest of honor is absent, silent, and unable to appreciate the tribute. The logistics of funerals are as complicated as weddings but with less time to plan – gathering mourners, ordering flowers, selecting readings, and arranging a ceremony. Senator John McCain was unusually forward thinking and accommodating as he orchestrated his memorial, relieving his family of the complexities of planning a state funeral. Whether or not you believe death is the end, a lack of preparation can create a hellish afterlife filled with legal and financial turmoil.

Take a cue from the Irish who celebrate death with a wake, a post-mortem gathering that honors and celebrates the deceased. If you know you're dying, or just because you never know, throw yourself a party. Why should others have all the fun?

> "Always go to other people's funerals, otherwise they
> won't come to yours." ~Yogi Berra

Conclusion

During the observation of an autopsy, it was clear the body was dead, not asleep. Even to an untrained observer, the cadaver's animating force had ceased. A pathologist's examination of the body can determine cause of death, the failure that disrupted biological life. If critical organs fail and can't be fixed, a person dies. Even an expertly wielded scalpel does not reveal intangibles like soul. Humans are mammals but imbued with a vital essence that extends beyond flesh. In the pathology suite, the dissected heart registered no residual love; the brain revealed no thoughts, hopes or dreams; and no organ corresponded to soul. Dissection identifies physiology and pathology; the knife does not expose connections, memories, or insights. Bodies are a vessel, not who we really are. Eventually, the form is outgrown and left behind.

Will it be a mad scramble and lingering uncertainties or a serene conclusion and good goodbye? How will I honor the life of the beloved? What would my loved one have wanted? Whose problem is it anyway? After all, the dead don't care. Take a different approach. If you love someone, or someone loves you, they'll be overwhelmed with sadness. Relieve their worries and ease burdens by planning, preparing, and informing ahead of time. The more decisions we make while we can, whether about donation or disposition, that's one less problem for the family to worry about. Without knowing preferences, your survivors will be forced to choose. The consequential decisions can have a lasting impact and all because you failed to share "What to know before I go …"

Reflections:

- How can I make things easier for everyone?
- If I have a strong preference regarding my body's disposition, have I told others or made plans?
- Have I made plans for my funeral? If so, are my plans and preferences in writing?
- Would I like a religious service and if so, do I have any requests for specific speakers or readings?

Actions:

- Donation: If you were an environmentalist in life, you may want to recycle in death. Contemplate the options: organ / tissue / whole body. Some restrictions apply.
- Disposition of remains: burial, cremation, or other? And will the remains get stored, scattered, or buried?
- Memorial or funeral? Religious service or big bash?
- Just in case you expect an ending where you go to sleep and don't wake up, make sure you've done the work so your death doesn't become a trauma for those who have to deal with it.

Resources:

- AARP resource pre-need funeral and burial laws: https://assets.aarp.org/rgcenter/consume/d17093_preneed.pdf
- Organ donation and religion: https://www.donatelife.net/organ-donation-and-religion/
- Costco caskets
  - Costco sells caskets as a service to Costco members. To verify availability and confirm shipping delivery time and date, call 1-800-955-2292. Or before placing your order, email customerservice@costco.com.
  - https://www.costco.com/must-read-this-important-information-before-purchasing-a-casket.product.11762743.html
- Monk-made caskets:
  - https://www.abbeycaskets.com/
  - https://trappistcaskets.com/caskets/
  - https://www.saintjosephabbey.com/view-the-caskets
- Green caskets:
  - https://www.memorials.com/green-caskets.php

TEN:

WEALTH

∞

GOOD STEWARDSHIP

I am blessed going in and going out.
All that I have are gifts.
Help me to be a good steward over all that has been
entrusted to my care.
I pray that everything that You have called me to do
will continue to prosper.
For all that I am and all that I have, I give thanks.
I am blessed to be a blessing to others.
As it was in the beginning and ever shall be… Deuteronomy 28

"We must remember we are stewards of what God
has provided for us, not owners." ~Joyce Meyers

My mother had been the one to manage family finances. When she died suddenly, my father did not know how much money they had, how much they owed, or even the location of the checkbook. When he found the checkbook, he discovered, "Oops, no money." The account was overdrawn. There were no funds when a lot of money was needed for hospital bills and funeral expenses. My husband and I didn't make much money as Army Second Lieutenants, but we were solvent. So, we ended up being the ones paying thousands of dollars for my mother's medical and death expenses.

Any financial planner will recommend that families stockpile funds for an emergency such as an unexpected car repair, sudden illness, or loss of employment. My parents were like most people – more month than money. When my mother died, family stepped in to help out. Not everyone's so lucky. These days, I'll read about people starting a GoFundMe site to pay for a funeral. At an emotionally fragile time of grief and high stress, adding one more thing can feel overwhelming. A lack of money compounds the misery. Funeral directors may be sympathetic, but their benevolence has limits. Mourners need to find a way to pay for the funeral, even if that means virtual panhandling.

A Tool for Good

How did you learn financial management? Were you actually taught, or was it just assumed you'd figure it out? Did you choose to follow your role models' examples? Or did you look at them and vow to take a different path?

Managing money is more than a math problem. It's easy for someone to say: "Spend less than you earn." That level of simplicity is no more helpful than telling someone who wants to lose weight: "Eat less and exercise more." As if that's all it takes. This isn't a book about financial planning, but in this chapter I'm urging you to think about our complicated relationship with money and why you should consider it as part of your end-of-life planning. You don't need a degree in finance to know these things:

- Money can be a tool for good.
- We work hard for our money.
- We can't take it with us.

Whatever your stage of life, a checkup with a financial advisor can help you make, or fine-tune, a financial plan that aligns with your values. A guide you trust can help clarify your thinking about your dreams and goals, and what steps and processes can help you accomplish them. Before you call a professional, think about what money means to you. Wealth has a spiritual aspect and is about more than numbers and assets: we trade life energy,[76] our time and creativity, in exchange for things we need or want. For example, we need food, but we have choices about what we eat and where we consume a meal. If you earn $15 dollars an hour and you buy a $15 pizza, you are trading one hour of your life energy for that meal. You don't have to be compulsive about expenses, but you need to realize that, "The price of anything is the amount of life you exchange for it."[77] The next time an impulse purchase beckons, consider calculating how many hours you'd need to work to cover the cost of that item. The reality of spending your life energy – using time rather than money as currency—may cause you to walk away from the transaction.

Consider your timeframe – now and in the future, during and after life. You want to protect your assets, ensuring you have enough to last

during your lifetime and to distribute the remainder to the people you
choose when you're dead.

- During: What do you want while you're alive for yourself and
  your loved ones? Will you have enough to support yourself from
  now through a span of unknown length and health?
- After: Do you want to pass on remaining assets after you no
  longer need them? Leaving a financial legacy requires planning
  beforehand to ensure your accumulation and possessions go to
  your intended beneficiaries.

Financial planning during life is about determining asset *allocation*,
an investment strategy that adjusts the percentage of assets in your portfolio, balancing goals, risk tolerance, and time horizon. This is beyond
the scope of this book and is between you and your financial advisor.

Estate planning is about ensuring asset *location*. This gets to the crux
of *Good Goodbyes*. Making things easier for your heirs helps contribute
to a good goodbye. Will your heirs know what you have and where to
find it? Don't send them on a scavenger hunt.

Asset *protection* is another thing to think about, during life and
after death. It's not only shielding valuables from creditors' claims or
lawsuits, but also considering how to distribute wealth in a way that
insulates heirs from risk, by preventing beneficiaries from squandering
their inheritance.

Set your intention to start getting your financial act together by
being prepared. Even if you consider yourself a smart money manager,
an advisor can act as a sounding board and provide guidance and
accountability. That person will look at what you have, estimate how
much you need, and give suggestions for bridging the gap. Based on
your age and health, an advisor can help you balance having enough

now while developing a plan for dispensing whatever is left over when you don't need it. It's your decision: who you'll give money to, when, how much, and for what purposes.

Have your plans in place early and not just because of compounding growth – the time value of money. Given the unreliability of crystal balls, it's better to be ready sooner rather than later. Don't wait. You'd hate to have good intentions waylaid by an unexpected early date with destiny. Meaning well doesn't work so well when your family is struggling in the aftermath of a predictably unpredictable event. Besides the time value of money, also consider the money value of time. Time invested now helps ensure asset location, so survivors have a map to your treasures rather than the frustration of a hunt and the uncertainty of not even knowing what exactly they're looking for. Pay love forward and save your loved ones from frantic searches for what you own or figuring out how to access assets when you're not around to guide them.

Remember: like other estate planning issues, money management can be complicated. Professionals undergo years of training, must pass qualifying exams, and operate under certifying boards' oversight. Consult a specialist for individualized guidance, especially if your specific case is tricky. *Good Goodbyes* aims to make you conversant, not fluent. Something is better than nothing, so make sure to have the minimum essentials completed. Think of it this way: we may consult Dr. Google for help identifying medical symptoms. However, most of us would hesitate to operate on ourselves while viewing a YouTube video for guidance.

Manage Money Mindfully

By itself, money is just printed paper—a good servant but a poor master.

Wise money management is more about a state of mind than a piece of paper. It's about taking control over your money rather than being controlled by it. Don't give money such importance that it rules, or ruins, your life. Money has transactional worth, but it's also an expression of values. What does money mean to you? Is it about earning, accumulating, and spending? Or security, status, and respect? Or about love, relationships, and independence? Is your spending aligned with your values? Most of us have a complicated relationship with money. For some, it almost verges on domestic violence, with desire and fear intertwined. We worry about having enough to ensure our physical necessities and material comforts, without stopping to consider how much we need for what purposes.

Looking at how we spend time and money gives insights into what we consider important. Acquiring possessions and cultivating a lifestyle are an expression of identity: who we are and how we see ourselves. Money can be a tool for living consciously and abundantly. It can provide opportunities for education, travel, or recreation. And, we can use it to bring beauty and wellbeing to the world as we share our bounty with others.

As spiritual beings having a human experience, we blend an outer, physical presence with an inner, spiritual essence. Physical is easier to recognize. Money is a simple benchmark. Access a bank account and your balance pops up. This number is a shorthand unit of measure for earthly success, which we may automatically connect to personal importance. Bill Gates' net worth may be substantially more than that of the man who approaches cars at a stoplight for a handout. But that's only part of the story. We should aim to balance a rich spiritual life with sufficient material possessions. Having enough means the ability to obtain physical necessities for survival: shelter, food, clothing, and transportation.

Currency is a unit of exchange. I give you dollars; in return, you might provide food, lodging, or transportation. Instead of viewing it as a business deal where money is traded for an object, it's possible to change our perspective and elevate the transaction to something sacred. It may be as simple as setting an intention and dedicating the money we spend to a higher purpose. Consecrating can transform: a blessing can turn bread into Communion, food into a feast shared with loved ones, or imbue the shelter over our heads into a home that safeguards and protects us from the elements. The right relationship with money looks at the bountiful results, rather than the quantity amassed. Remember that not everything that counts can be counted.

As I've been writing *Good Goodbyes*, my husband and I have been working with a financial planning team. As we approach a transitional time in our lives, we're committed to getting our act together – to walk the talk I'm suggesting in this book. During this assessment, we developed these financial planning goals:

- Smart: Ensure we have enough for the remainder of our life. The holy grail is balancing optimizing investments and minimizing taxes, knowing that a greater return will result in more taxes. Evaluate insurance to ensure it's sufficient.
- Simple: Consolidate, reduce, and clean up accounts. Minimize mutual fund and credit card redundancies. Make things easier for our son (who's currently active duty and our executor), if and when he has to settle our estate.
- Legacy-oriented: Develop a more systematic approach for gifting and charitable contributions.

Simplify Your Assets

Will your survivors have enough to stay in their home? In the aftermath of death, don't leave loved ones fearful about whether they can afford their current lifestyle. You want to mitigate your loved ones' burdens, not add to their distress. Anxiety and uncertainty will compound bereavement.

Take stock. A budget can give you a baseline. Knowing what's coming in and going out points to possibilities. Our money choices have benefits and costs. Without a spending plan, it's easy to piddle small amounts away, leaving nothing meaningful or memorable behind.

Do you have enough for as long as you shall live? Is it available to use without liquidating assets? You're responsible for the quality of your life. By having a plan, you can make sure you have enough to take care of yourself without draining your family's resources or relying on the kindness of state or strangers.

Cash Flow: Tracking the Ins and Outs

What do you own and owe? Decide what needs to be paid, closed, or cancelled. Create a master list of your assets, debts, and accounts. Ensure paper and digital access. Check the list occasionally and revise when needed.

- What comes in? Include wages and earnings, pensions, military or government retirement, annuities, alimony, and social security.
- What goes out? Include recurring bills, such as a mortgage payment (or rent), loans, credit card(s), entertainment, charities, etc. What bills are paid automatically? How do bills get paid? How much do you pay, on what frequency?

- Write down account numbers and the locations of accounts.
- Properly designate property. Some items pass outside your Will. Examples include: beneficiary designation for life insurance policies, IRAs, or 401(k) accounts. Go the extra step to verify the right people will inherit your assets.

Treasure Chest: An Accumulation You Can Count On

- Bank accounts
- Stocks
- Mutual funds
- Investments
- Retirement accounts (IRAs, 401(k)s)
- Real property: property deeds, vehicle titles

Create a Safety Net

Life happens. Consider the possibilities and prepare. Financial planners suggest having at least three to six months of living expenses stockpiled for rainy days. Emergency funds will help pay bills in the event of a hardship – job loss, medical emergency, car repair.

Insurance to mitigate risk should also be part of your portfolio. It helps protect assets in the event of calamities, like accidents or disaster. Insurance transfers the cost of solving a problem in exchange for a fee. There are enough varieties and options to make your head spin. A prudent step would be to consult an agent to assess and determine: What do you have? What do you need? Is it enough? Some basic types include health insurance, which covers medical costs. A homeowner's or renter's policy insures your home and possessions. If you own a vehicle, auto insurance protects you, your vehicle, and anyone injured in an accident involving your car. An umbrella policy covers costs in excess of your vehicle and homeowners policies. Long-term care insurance provides for residential or in-home nursing care. Life insurance can provide financial security for loved ones upon your death.

With long-term care coverage, it's not just a matter of whether you might need it, but also whether you can you afford it. If you have assets, you might figure that self-insuring makes financial sense. An insurance agent who specializes in long-term care shared her perspective on why you might want to rethink this option. In her experience, those who self-insure are often NOT willing to spend the money on caregiving when the time comes, resulting in the healthier spouse stepping in. This can be a recipe for disaster if the caregiver is also at a vulnerable age. And don't think you can count on Medicaid for nursing home care. It's a safety net last resort. To qualify, a person can own a home, a car and have no more than $2000 in the bank.

Optimize Your Legacy

"You should leave your children enough so they can do anything, but not enough so they can do nothing." ~Warren Buffett

Shirtsleeves to shirtsleeves in three generations is a financial planning adage. One generation starts with nothing but amasses wealth due to hard work and initiative. By the time their great-grandchildren take over, the family is sometimes back where they started, with little or nothing. Wealth passed down from grandparents and parents can be a blessing, providing the good fortune of a trust fund. But, it can also become a burden, when recipients expect an easy path without needing to work hard. Family members who lack direction or ambitions may have difficulty managing a generous windfall. To protect your children from themselves or from relationships that terminate, a trust with a spendthrift provision helps protect assets.

Money can be a force for good, or not. It can bring families together or tear them apart. We are responsible for managing our personal assets and protecting the Earth's resources. Whatever riches we've been entrusted with – wealth, health, friends, or talents – it's up to us to make the most of what we have. Being a good steward implies responsible planning and management of resources to ensure they are used in the most beneficial way.

Unhappiness may come from short-term thinking: trading what we want in the moment for what we want most. When there's no plan, financial decisions are often made impulsively, in a vacuum, without evaluating the opportunity costs. Every choice has a trade-off and limits access to alternatives. Money tied up in one endeavor prevents potential gain from other possible prospects.

Conclusion

It always seems too soon, until it's too late. With death as certainty, each of us must define the path that's best for us. Money planning is an essential strand of end-of-life planning. Gaining control over financial affairs requires a process to optimize monetary benefits. In the event of incapacity or death, you want your loved ones to know what to do, who to call for assistance, and where important documents are located. To a large extent, you can minimize a lot of family angst by developing a thorough estate plan.

We will leave behind a legacy. It's not only something for world leaders or celebrities to think about. And, it's not just the ending, but what we do along the way. What did you contribute? How did you inspire? Did you care enough to make your afterlife less burdensome for others? Getting your affairs in order is your final love letter for survivors. Composing it requires imagination – a future orientation for a time when you're not around. And empathy—considering what it will be like for the person tasked as your executor. Your efforts now will pay off later as love in action. Adopt "no surprises, no disasters" as your estate planning mantra. Adding a spiritual dimension to money management will bring richness to your life. If you believe that all that we have is a gift, consider how to steward these blessings in a manner that is consistent with the passion, purpose, and values with which we live. Let it be said: "Well done good and faithful servant."[78]

Reflections:

- Is your spending aligned with your values?
- What do you want while you're alive for yourself and your loved ones?
- Will you have enough to support yourself (and your spouse)—from now through a span of unknown length and health?
- Do you want to pass on remaining assets intentionally after you no longer need them?

Actions:

Leave a trace by preparing your asset location list:
- In: What comes in each month? (Income)
- Out: What do you owe? Track and record recurring expenses.
- Own: What are your treasures? Inventory high value assets.

Resources:

Before you consult a lawyer, check out information on estate planning
https://www.nolo.com/legal-encyclopedia/wills-trusts-estates

Eleven

Digital

∞

Virtual Immortality

"When something goes out on the Internet, it's out there forever."[79]

My friend's husband, JC, died in 2017. His widow, Donna, has had to keep his phone active since then to be able to access his Google account, including emails. She didn't know the passwords and to change login information would require a court order – not the easiest fix. Accessing some financial accounts requires two-factor authentication—using JC's phone. Some emails, like from the Washington Mystics basketball team or Starbucks awards, have never worked right going to their other email account. Recently, Donna had to log in to the electric utility account when the auto-payment platform changed. Since she didn't have the password, she clicked "Forgot my password." But her answers to the security question: "What is your pet's name?" didn't work. Next step: the dreaded phone call to customer service. She planned for a nightmare, thinking she'd just say her husband couldn't remember, not that he was dead. What she discovered: the account was in both names and the representative was very nice, staying on the phone until everything was fixed. Donna said: "You wouldn't believe the problems some members of my bereavement support group have had." She went on to suggest: "Have things in both names."

Don't worry about whether life will end up being a sprint or a marathon. We have only limited control over its length. What most people don't seem to realize is that life *is* a relay race – a runner finishing one leg passes the baton to the next person. You are the first runner. The baton represents a generational transfer of vital information and valuable assets. And it's your job to make sure that the handoff goes as smoothly as possible to whoever is on the receiving end. In the scheme of things, a track meet isn't that important; a dropped baton may disqualify a team or influence their finish. It may be devastating in the moment but has limited long-term impact. Not so in real life; your system, preparation, and practice will ensure the baton passes smoothly. Timely actions can have a lasting effect on the people you love.

A map, a chest, and a key are what you need to provide to your survivors. You don't want them stumbling and fumbling in the dark. You want your family knowing what to do and where to find the treasure. Don't bungle it; you may not get a second chance. The award for a clean handoff will be finishing well and peace of mind.

A Map

You've concealed your assets and hidden clues to where the treasure is buried—great thinking from a security perspective. Someday you intend to draw a map listing accounts and passwords – a good intention unless you don't get around to it before the information dies with you. Without you or a map to guide their efforts, your loved ones will probably end up searching and digging indiscriminately. When they eventually give up, they'll wonder what they've missed and question why you made things so painful. In fictional accounts, a treasure map identifies the location of the pirates' chest of buried valuables. In real life, you may want to consider leaving a record to help your survivors find your wealth. Being cagey or leaving secretive tips will make for a frustrating hunt. Just be direct – if you love them and trust them. Even if your treasure consists of values and stories rather than valuables or stocks, be a gracious and proactive giver.

Your actions matter. Your estate isn't the wilderness. "Leave no trace" makes ethical sense in the outdoors, but not for your survivors. Getting lost in the back-country can be scary and disorienting. Being lost in a mess of papers can be maddening and unproductive. Don't subject your loved ones to a scavenger hunt, where they don't know where to go or what to do. To minimize heartache and negative impacts when you depart, leave a trace, so future generations can appreciate your legacy. Draw a treasure map and orient your survivors. Make lists and leave directions for others, to include the location of vital documents; beneficiaries of life insurance policies, your fiduciary agent for bank accounts and bill paying, and let survivors know who inherits real property, who cares for your children, where pets will go, and final arrangements. You may also want to leave instructions for handling social media accounts. Your loved ones will need access to key financial information, passwords to electronic records, and access to electronic devices. It's advisable to keep both written documentation and digital files. Store listings, logins, and numbers someplace secure yet accessible. The master lists you leave behind will minimize frustration and maximize peace of mind.

A Chest

At one time, girls received hope chests for storing essential home goods, such as linens, towels, and quilts, in preparation for marriage. Having a designated chest allowed for the gradual collection of necessities, so young women entered marriage equipped to start a household. This piece of furniture was almost sacramental, a tangible sign symbolizing hope – for finding a partner, for loving relationships, for living a full life. Wedding registries and online shopping make the idea of hope chests seem quaint today, since if you want it, you can buy it or someone else will. As originally intended, hope chests may be a thing of the past, but every adult needs the modern version—a Legacy Treasure Chest—as a place to store vital documents. What goes in your chest? Consider it a just-in-case container to hold important items you'd grab-and-go if you had to evacuate in a hurry. Specifically, you'll want to store medical, legal, and financial documents that would be hard to replace, including titles and deeds, birth certificates, marriage license, military discharge papers, shot records, insurance policies, and passports. Include paper versions and/or digital files. These days, many vital records have been digitized, but it would take an effort to retrieve and reconstruct documents you lost. Tangible valuables might include special jewelry, diplomas, family mementoes, photos, and external hard drives.

You might already have a locked box or safe – some sort of fire-proof metal container. An alternative is a bank safe deposit box. In any case, make sure someone knows where the box is and how to access it. Keep health directives handy or uploaded to the cloud. In the moment of need, have them easy to retrieve. Safeguard the original copy of your Will – the only version that will work when filing for probate—but make sure people identified in the document, such as executor or guardian, have copies. Think of the catch-22 scenario that might crop up for your designated helpers, if your executor has trouble accessing your safety deposit box to obtain that document that identifies him or her as the person authorized to retrieve the papers. Make it simple and minimize the roadblocks for those who have agreed to help.

The Key

You've prepared the treasure map. Your valuables are in a protected stronghold. Don't forget to provide the key that will open the lock. Balance digital integrity with accessibility. It may sound contradictory, ensuring privacy and security as well as understandable and retrievable paperwork. Make sure your digital assets are:

- Secure: Safeguard important documents to maintain privacy.
- Accessible: Ensure that important papers are available when needed by those who need to know.
- Current: Keep personal and financial information up-to-date.

Identity security: It could be as simple as losing your wallet, an emotionally traumatic event with possible legal and financial repercussions. If someone steals personal information, the thief may use it to commit fraud, such as applying for credit, emptying bank accounts, filing a tax return to obtain a refund, or obtaining medical services. If you are victimized, it will cost you time and money to clear your name and repair your credit. Credit history not only impacts your ability to borrow money, it can also hurt job prospects or housing options.

Digital protection: Awareness and prevention are the best ways to fight financial fraud and identity theft. Unless you've had accounts hacked, the protection of data and passwords may sound like "blah, blah, blah" or one more thing to add to the nagging task list. Incapacity or post-mortem can be prime times for identity theft issues. The lag between the reporting of a death and updating of records at financial institutions, credit bureaus, and the Social Security Administration provides criminals with time to "ghost" your identity and make a mess of financial accounts. Securing accounts or catching suspicious attempts early can save you from identity theft and its collateral damage.

Password protection: Anyone with an online presence has numerous passwords to remember. Every account needs a different password because if a hacker manages to get access to one account, it can compromise other accounts that use the same password. You want your passwords complicated and hard to guess—for others—but easy for you to remember and retrieve. Criminals want what you have, so make it as hard as possible for them. At least, consider using a password manager or multifactor authentication (requires entering a separately sent code to log into an account). You've heard this before: for your digital protection, use strong, unique passwords, institute multifactor authentication, and regularly review your credit information. Back up your data on storage devices or in the cloud.

Digital Afterlife

Social media accounts may not be the main priority after a loved one has died, but they can add pain in months after a death. Sometimes getting a reminder to post a birthday greeting on your deceased friend's wall can trigger fresh grief. Or you may see it as an opportunity to remember that they are missed and not forgotten. Some survivors keep social media accounts active so friends can share thoughts and memories. Shared expressions of sorrow can help make sense of a loss, bringing comfort and condolences. Transitioning a social media account to a memorial page feels less final than deleting it outright.

Honor the deceased person's wishes. Did they include details in their Will or letter or instruction regarding what they'd like to happen to social media accounts? If not, you may want to visit the accounts and save certain posts and photos. Err on the side of caution: if you're not sure whether to save something, save it anyway. At a later date, it can be deleted, but once an account has been deleted, the contents are gone forever. As with your own online presence, be careful about what you share and who you share it with.

A Story From the Trenches

For most people, the transition from life to death is *not* going to be "here today, gone tomorrow." The end is more likely to be a rollercoaster ride – with intermittent moments of lucidity and health, interspersed with episodes of waning strength and fuzzy thinking. One way to avoid a guardianship situation is to complete a durable power of attorney (PoA) and appoint someone to oversee financial and legal matters. Preparing the legal documents requires necessary steps, but these must go hand-in-hand with ensuring the designated individuals are willing and able to act in your stead. Be clear that it could require a significant amount of work.

MK and her husband had agreed to act as their friend's financial proxy. They didn't expect to be called into service so soon, but shortly after being designated, their friend experienced an incapacitating medical event. After a year of helping their friend and with no end in sight, here are some insights from their experiences.

1. Passwords: Make sure your PoA has your passwords. Yes, you want to be careful about security, but if you trust someone to represent you, you need to trust them with access to accounts. If you keep digital documents and your computer is password-protected, your agents need the password. It doesn't do much good to have a comprehensive list stored on an inaccessible machine.

2. Assets and bills: What do you own? What do you owe? Compile a list of accounts: bank, credit, investment, household. Also, what bills get paid on what schedule? Recurring monthly expenses might include phone, utilities, or credit cards. Some bills may be on a quarterly (water, sewer, trash) or annual cycle (taxes or subscriptions). It's not enough to know when bills are due, but also what's the process for paying them (credit card, recurring debit, mail a check, etc.)? Are any bills paid automatically? Your PoA needs to know.

3. Communication: Maybe one friend is the financial proxy and another person is the medical agent. Divide-and-conquer with discrete areas of responsibility seems appropriate until the medical decision-maker needs to know whether there's money to pay for supplementary therapy, not covered by insurance. The team of helpers may unintentionally be working at odds with each other without a "quarterback" in charge. What happens if there's a difference of opinion? How would a disagreement get resolved?

4. Sounding board: Having another person to discuss things with and ask questions to can be a blessing. Most people don't do this work often enough to develop competence.

5. Bottom line: The best laid plans will have gaps and loopholes. Do the best you can. You are acting in good faith, doing your best, and doing your friend a favor. Love in action.

Last Words

Eventually something will happen to you or your loved ones. Humans are mortal; your internet existence can be immortal. If you're going to live forever online, make sure you're happy with your digital presence. Don't make it harder than it needs to be for another person to access your accounts. Let a trusted individual know accounts, logins, and passwords.

Getting digital affairs in order is a lot of work, *almost* making cleaning the garage or clearing the basement seems like fun by comparison. After you're gone and facing a heavenly accounting, your loved ones will be subjected to an earthly accounting on your behalf. You can make it easier or harder for them. Failing to provide the map, chest, and key will complicate things, like dropping people you love in the wilderness without navigation tools and proper gear. You want your legacy to be both memorable and positive. The more planning and preparation you do ahead of time will make a difference, so settling your affairs is less grueling and more grace-filled. Is that too much to ask? Don't leave it to chance and compound catastrophe.

Reflections:

- If I got hit by a bus and someone needed to assume responsibility for my affairs tomorrow, is that person identified and is the system "plug-and-play"?

- What if a few hours of work made a difference for your survivors? Would you be willing to do it?
- What's my preference for having immortal social media and email accounts?
- Are the people who need to know familiar with the location of my treasure map and legacy chest? Will they be able to find things without significant searching?
- From the perspective of the people who will need to clear my home after I'm gone, have I considered how easy or hard it will be for them?

Actions:

- Create a master list. Starting today, as bills arrive, compile a list of what you owe and how you pay. Include user names, passwords, and PINs. Collect logins for email, internet, financial accounts, cloud storage, and social media, and PINs for computer, phone, and ATM. Review your list frequently, revise as needed, and print after you update it.
- Recognize that missing a bill like an insurance premium may get the policy cancelled.
- Scan important documents and photos.
- Keep a copy of all essential documents, an account list, and a password list on a thumb USB drive or external hard drive. Password protect each file or set up a password on the storage device itself.
- Reduce or consolidate accounts. Make it simple for both yourself and anyone who has to assume your digital and financial life after you die.

- Secure accounts by using strong, unique passwords or a password manager. Some accounts now require multifactor authentication. According to *Consumer Reports*, if you do just one thing, set up multifactor authentication.
- Set up alerts on your existing accounts, so you get notified about a large transaction or password change.
- Make a list of what you carry around with you in you purse or wallet (ID cards, credit cards, etc) in case they are lost or stolen.
- Monitor your credit reports. Once a year, you can get free copies of credit reports at www.annualcreditreport.com.
- If you think you may be a victim of identity theft, find solutions at https://securityplanner.consumerreports.org/tool/get-help-with-identity-theft.
- Your digital fitness is not one-and-done. You need to review and revise documents periodically, and especially if you experience a significant life change like a move, divorce, or cognitive decline.

Resources:

- ID Theft: https://www.usa.gov/identity-theft; https://helpcenter.idtheftcenter.org/s/
- Free fraud alert service at Experian, TransUnion, or Equifax can monitor your credit for 90 days. In the event that you or someone else tries to set up a new account or take out a loan, you'll be contacted to confirm your identity.
- Consumer Reports Security Planner: https://securityplanner.consumerreports.org/action-plan/1JoWC0F9DMwiVK18d_wCi4U7

TWELVE:

SHARE

∞

YOUR LOVE LETTER TO THE FUTURE

"There was never yet an uninteresting life. Such a thing is an impossibility. Inside of the dullest exterior there is a drama, a comedy, and a tragedy." ~Mark Twain

Becky, my first West Point roommate, fought the death sentence to her last breath. She wasn't convicted of wrongdoing; her body betrayed her. Afflicted with Lou Gehrig's disease (Amyotrophic Lateral Sclerosis [ALS]), a progressive neurological illness, activities we take for granted, such as walking, talking, swallowing, and breathing, gradually disappeared. Becky understood that she wouldn't survive. As ALS progressively robbed her of the ability to perform activities of daily living, she tried to slow, fight, and beat the disease.

While ALS stole her physical abilities, Becky persisted. She learned to communicate with blinks, translated by a tele-pad and displayed on the screen or spoken in a mechanized voice. She partnered with others in the ALS community to draft legislation, present solutions, and offer comfort. Although her body was paralyzed, she continued seeking a cure for ALS, efforts that included arranging for the post-mortem donation of her brain for research purposes. Her efforts were recognized on the death certificate, which listed her occupation as "ALS Advocate."

Most of us do a lot of pretending, imagining death as some remote event that can be delayed indefinitely. Becky didn't have that luxury. She understood: "It's time to wrap things up." With help from another West Point classmate, Becky completed estate documents and gave instructions. Mementoes retrieved from storage led to reminiscing. She was preparing for her last journey.

Leave a Treasure Map

A red folder labeled "Emergency Procedures" caught my eye on the clinic counter as I was making a follow-up appointment. That's what we need: individualized emergency procedures with a clear checklist that will guide others in a crisis – no fumbling around when minutes count. If you're not able to help due to incapacity, make sure that others know what to do, how to find your Living Will or Will or gain access to a safe. As you've been reading *Good Goodbyes*, you've had the opportunity to consider what matters to you:

- You're Aware. You've decided what you want based on the reality of what mortal beings face.
- You're Prepared. You've documented your wishes, inventoried the property you own, and know how you want to dispose of it.

- Now Share. It's not just that a job isn't done until the paperwork is finished. It's also a matter of discussing what you have decided and documented. You want to make sure the people who need to know, actually *do* know – your wishes and the location of your valuable papers and tangible valuables without a massive search and major headaches. Make it easy for the ones you love.

And you also want to share what you learned and what was important to you. Traditional estate planning focuses on wealth – inventorying, protecting, and transferring financial assets. We are much more than the things we've accumulated or even awards, titles, or fame we've earned. Years after you have walked the earth, people will want to know about you – your personal legacy and the parts of your life that made you, you.

Leave a Legacy

"Not everything that counts can be counted."[80]

Cindy was pregnant when she was diagnosed with cancer. Her child was a toddler when she died. When she realized that the hoped-for miracle was unlikely, Cindy set a goal: to make sure her children remembered her. She chose hospice care for the last months of her life and set about building and recording memories with the remaining time. The announcement that the end was near gave her the motivation to look back and examine life's meaning. She also looked ahead, knowing that earthly time was winding down. Cindy understood, "It's now or never," and set about recording videos, assembling photo albums, and writing notes for loved ones, until cancer spread to her brain. She wasn't afraid to die, even though hearts were breaking at the impending separation. Cindy chose to live fully until the end.

If you love someone, you don't just leave. You say something, send a text, or write a note before heading out the door. If you didn't, your loved ones would certainly worry or wonder: "Did we matter so little that you didn't say something?" The body doesn't last, but connections will continue. When you're gone, make sure you're not forgotten. Stories not told will disappear. Most of us won't have biographers eager to research us. So, it's up to us. The bonus of doing it yourself is that you'll get to craft the narrative the way you want. Having a conversation about death—personal, not abstraction—will take courage. You have to decide whether Love is greater than Fear. Are you willing to pay love forward by sharing?

Talking about death and dying makes for a daunting conversation. One way to mitigate the anxiety is to talk before dark clouds start gathering on the horizon. Perhaps, ask someone else to help facilitate the discussion to ease the emotional impact. In messages for family and friends, say any things that need to be said, but always include the magic words: "Thank you. I love you. Forgive me. I forgive you. Goodbye." Start now in order to make them a habit. Make a practice of saying them in person, so when it is the last time, you don't go without saying goodbye. Last words are lasting words.

Life Review

"We had the experience but missed the meaning."[81]

Make peace with your past by reviewing your life. Look back and consider the highlights: memories of childhood; turning points; happiest and hardest moments; adventures; principles you lived by;

values and beliefs; life lessons and mistakes; roads taken and not taken; hopes, dreams, and aspirations for future generations. Every life is unique and worthy of preservation for generations yet to be. Financial assets will be spent and forgotten, but your legacy can provide priceless inheritance.

Don't let the stories die with you. One aspect of legacy involves telling your story. Remembering and writing about your life helps to distill meaning. If we ignore or deny the reality of death, we won't have the opportunity to pass on our legacy or write our stories. It doesn't have to be a book-length memoir, because as journalist Tim Russert observed, "Someday your entire life will be summed up in twenty minutes."[82] And don't expect that your social media posts will have staying power. Mostly, they're here today and gone tomorrow, unless you happen to run for or hold public office. Special programs like StoryCorps or the Veterans History Project help facilitate the collection of personal stories. The Library of Congress-sponsored Veterans History Project offers a Field Kit with instructions and interview questions.

Your life mattered. What was important to you? Looking back, think about how you want to be remembered. Looking forward, consider the life experiences and beliefs you want to pass on. In the crafting of your legacy include:

- Lessons learned – What messages will you leave behind?
- Light spread – What light did you bring to the world?
- Love shared – Who did you love?

Last matters: Living Into the Vision

> I'm sorry that I didn't find out what prompted
> my parents to immigrate to the U.S.

Or what it was like for them growing up
in large farming families in Ireland.
Or how they reconnected in New York City,
a meeting that eventually led to marriage.

People will write or say nice things about you when you're dead (or if you think they won't, you may want to work on fixing that while you have the chance). Memorial tributes will attempt to condense your life into 1000 words or less, a 15–20-minute speech. Often, the stories and details get lost. Our unique light is not extinguished when we die; it shines on, but in many cases without the particulars that would speak to our essential essence.

If you read obituaries (obits) in the newspaper, you may be drawn to fascinating vignettes more than biographical details. Certain essays make me wish that I had known the featured person. But without fail, if there's a photo, the person is smiling. How should I interpret the happy demeanor? Is the death experience better than expected? Does the grin hint at "I know a secret and I'm not telling"? What has been revealed in the afterlife? Without knowing the context, it may be less about something the deceased knows that we don't and more that someone else picked out a particular photo that speaks to a happier time.

An obit is a summary statement, your life's highlights reel. It's usually written by someone else who has decided what's important about your life. Instead of leaving it to chance, write your own memorial article, or at least provide an outline with the basics. Who better to provide the details of your life than you? Use it as a blueprint to inspire and motivate – an aspirational document. What will I do with my remaining time? What dreams do I hope to fulfill in the time remaining? What's on my bucket list? What am I most proud of? Who will I be leaving behind? What's the vision for the rest of my life? If you have a goal you want to accomplish, seize this moment to share: Here's what I loved; This is what I accomplished; I'm leaving the world a better place because of _____. There's no living without risking.

We often wait until someone dies before we tell them how much they have meant to us. The word *eulogy* derives from Greek and means praise; however, people generally associate a eulogy with funerals. We remember and tell stories when the guest of honor is unable to bask in the love and appreciation offered.

The message engraved on your gravestone will sum up your story for eternity. Consider this blank slate as your final act of creation. What will be your message for the ages? What do you want others to remember? Who did you love? How did you live? Is there a quotation or motto that summarizes your life's philosophy? You can make changes until the final date is carved in stone.

People who have been revived after a near-death experience recall going through a life review, with significant episodes flashing before their eyes. Don't wait for that possibility. Although we are destined to die, the narrative can live on. Unless you tell the story, write the poem, or assemble the album with photos and captions, information about who we were and what was important to us will be lost. Without effort, the memories will fade. That sage for the ages Dr. Seuss reminds: "Sometimes you will never know the value of a moment, until it becomes a memory."

Reflections:

- What do you want people to remember about you?
- How do you want to reach out to future generations?

- During your life, what did you come to see or know clearly? What was revealed to you? How did your perspective expand or shift?

Actions:

- Find a support and accountability partner. Having someone to do the work with will help overcome fear and procrastination.
- Don't wait. Tell your stories now. Write them down.
- Start by writing a single chapter of your life's history. Create a table of contents based on stages, turning points, or stepping stones. Give each chapter a descriptive title. What would you call the current chapter?
- Record a soundtrack for your life. Choose lyrics that resonate. If you and your beloved have a special song, include that melody.
- Compose an ethical Will so future generations will know what you valued and how you made a difference. Inspire others with your amazing resilience and kindness.
- Write your obit. Starting with biographical information may feel less threatening:
  - Full name
  - Nickname
  - Date / place of birth
  - Parents' names
  - Notable youth info: Sports, scouts, or other activities
  - High school / graduation year
  - Noteworthy Activities
  - Military service

- Summary of career
- Military medals / decorations
- Summary of civilian career – include places / dates
- Noteworthy / favorite job
- Retirement date
- Hobbies / travels / philanthropic works / memberships / honors / recognitions
- Full name of spouse
- Marriage date/place
- Names of family members
- Where you intend to be buried/interred
- Favorite charity

Resources:

- The Conversation Project https://theconversationproject.org/
- StoryCorps https://storycorps.org/
- Veterans History Project https://www.loc.gov/vets/kit.html
- StoryWorth: Write your life story a week at a time www.storyworth.com/questions

THIRTEEN:

CARE

∞

KEEP IN MIND THE BOTTOM LINE

"There is a land of the living and a land of the dead and the bridge is love, the only survival, the only meaning."[83]

O ur greatest gift is love. If you lead with your heart and keep love in mind as the bottom line, other actions and decisions will fall into place. Love can override fear, procrastination, apathy, and inertia. It can elevate "getting affairs in order" from distasteful chore to heart mission and urgent status.

We share because we care. Love is not only a feeling; it's also a decision. We get one chance to get dying right. One of the most important aspects of demonstrating caring is having open, ongoing conversations. Being aware of what you value and sharing your goals are a gift that will help you and the ones you love. Some people find speaking about death—their own demise—threatening and offensive. One way to start the process is by taking baby steps. Talking early and often, before there's an illness, diagnosis, or hospitalization, can remove some of the apprehension. If someone objects to talking about their end-of-life preferences, start by explaining what you've decided for yourself. And then, tell them why you're asking: "Because I care about you, I want to make sure that I will honor what you want, but first I need to know what that is. Your planning ahead makes it easier for both of us." We're inclined to avoid difficult conversations, so discussing illness, decline, and dying can feel awkward. We may even worry that talking about dying will make it happen. The people closest to us do not always agree on what might be the best course of action, but it's better to know about disagreements ahead of time. We can help mediate differences and educate everyone so that decisions are based on the best information possible. We can only break through the delusion of plenty of time by normalizing the process of having the conversations and getting life documents done. Exposing ourselves to what we fear lessens its power over us. It will always seem too soon until it's too late.

By looking to the past and reflecting on where forgiveness may be needed, and by looking to the future and providing guidance and messages for friends and family, we can leave behind a legacy of love, forgiveness, and gratitude. It's up to you. How will you answer: Is my love for others greater than fear, inertia, and superstition? As life comes to an end, death will not take the love shared, the bonds with others, and memories experienced. As Morrie Schwartz's wise words remind: "Death ends a life, not a relationship. All the love you created is still there. All the memories are still there. You live on—in the hearts of everyone you have touched and nurtured while you were here."[84]

"When it's over, I don't want to wonder if I have made of my life something particular, and real."[85]

On the morning she died, Becky blinked a message that displayed on her telepad: "Love you all. Bye-bye." That particular time didn't seem much different from any others during the course of her disease, but it ended up being the last. For five years, Becky had proven to be a survivor, overcoming setbacks and enduring suffering. Becky had stayed engaged with her causes – spending time with family and friends, seeking a cure for ALS, and improving the world around her. Her legacy and last message continue to comfort her family. When those who loved Becky reflect on her life, they may forget the negative aspects of her disease but will remember the courage she exhibited and the love she expressed.

Time inexorably counts down. We will never be younger or have more time than right now. Ensure your important papers are accessible, understandable, legal, and secure. Tomorrow's generation depends on today's preparation. While you can, pass on the story of who you were, including what your loved ones meant to you, challenges faced, and lessons learned. Share because you care. In his book *Being Mortal*, Dr. Gawande elaborates on life's meaning:

> In the end, people don't view their life as merely the average of all its moments – which, after all, is mostly nothing much plus some sleep. For human beings, life is meaningful because it is a story. A story has a sense of a whole, and its arc is determined by the significant moments, the ones where something happens. Measurements of people's minute-by-minute levels of pleasure and pain miss this fundamental aspect of human existence. A

seemingly happy life may be empty. A seemingly difficult life may be devoted to a great cause. We have purposes larger than ourselves.[86]

We never know when a last time might be the last. In the ballad *Beautiful Boy*, John Lennon sings about a future with his 5-year-old son, more poignant because Lennon was shot and killed later that year. As the song reminds us life happens. Seize the joy and prioritize the present. But also, be intentional about your vision for the future. Live with the end in mind. In the end what matters will be the lives touched and connections made. Until the final date is carved in stone, we have opportunities to revise our legacy and remember that what remains is more than a perishable body. Don't go without saying goodbye.

FOURTEEN

COMPLETION

∞

EVERY ENDING IS ALSO A BEGINNING

You can't go back and change the beginning but you can start where you are and change the ending.[87]

After prayers for the young man in the ICU, devastated family and friends tiptoed out, having chosen not to witness the final steps. Trauma that had brought the patient to the hospital was unfixable; medicine failed to restore functioning and prevent death. The nurse silenced alarms and turned off monitors. By removing the ventilator, she disconnected the breathing apparatus that had kept the body "alive." Holding the patient's hand as the nurse switched off the dials and withdrew tubes, I watched his face and prayed for the repose of his soul. With the machines off, his chest stilled. Not even a residual gasp escaped; the brain injury had completely interrupted the body's impulses to pump and breathe. Color drained from his cheeks and temperature cooled with the stopping of mechanical "life" force. The nurse charted the time of death for posterity. Spirit had returned to Mystery, leaving behind a souvenir of incarnation.

What?

Anytime we head out the door, there's no assurance that we'll return. Life includes a death sentence, with a no-money-back guarantee or warranties on broken parts. We are born pregnant with death. A countdown started at birth; time remaining gets smaller each day, as an individualized gestational period unspools to a common terminus. The one-way ticket issued at birth offers no clues about the length of the journey or adventures to be experienced. We focus on the form – lavishing attention on bodies – the most tangible aspect, but also the most vulnerable. Science can keep bodies alive longer than the people who inhabit them. Our lack of anticipation and preparation leads to overreliance on the prevailing medical-technical model, singularly focused on keeping the body operating. As life ends, we become combatants in a never-ending battle to maintain vital signs, even as vitality wanes or vanishes. Impermanence is demonized, as we fantasize that, given sufficient resources and scientific breakthroughs, we can eliminate our terminal fate.

So What?

Death reminds us about our common humanity and fate. Wealth, power, or fame accumulated during mortal lives will disappear when each person crosses the threshold back to eternity. Death comes, bringing conclusion, although not necessarily completion. We know how the story ends, and if we take advantage, we can draft the closing chapter ourselves, taking the opportunity to reflect on what matters most, summarize legacy, reconcile relationships, ask forgiveness, say thanks, and express love. In our ignorance, we conclude that what we call "life" is total reality without realizing it's just a vacation in a corporeal time share. Like a tourist whose visa expires, eventually it's time to go home. We passed through to learn lessons, bring light to the world, and make a difference.

Now What?

Fullness of life involves more than maintenance of body parts. No navigation device or app provides an optimal route or warns of potholes on the journey, or even confirms that the destination exists. Failing to plan results in a chaotic conclusion. Getting your end-of-life act together can bring peace of mind, ease burdens, and be a love letter that lasts. For end of life to be a transformative passage rather than a medical crisis requires connecting to Spirit, being Aware, being Prepared, and Sharing because you Care. Keeping love in mind as the bottom line can help us move from good intentions to thoughtful actions.

Spirit: The premise behind *Good Goodbyes* is that humans are spiritual beings who temporarily inhabit bodies. Eventually the human experience ends, and we return to Source. We can encounter that threshold intentionally or accidentally. If you wish to live a purposeful life, consider your line in the sand. What do you value? What matters most? What feeds your soul? Honoring your spiritual essence means choosing to live with a sense of the sacred.

Aware: We can run but we can't hide. Our date with destiny lies ahead. Being aware lets us face the future with facts, not fear. We can deal with most things, as long as we know what we're dealing with. The laws of nature apply to us. As bodies start failing, we need to shift from medical cures to healing relationships and eliciting a sense of completion. We have a *deadline*, and all *saves* are temporary. Neither access to care nor providers' skills will prevent death. While our outcome is absolute, being prepared can minimize suffering and ensure peace. In the end, moments will have mattered more than metrics.

Prepare: Fix the roof while the sun is shining. Don't wait for the storm to batter the house before acting. Take the initiative before disaster strikes. Be prepared: pay attention to detail, think through options, and anticipate problems. Whether death will be a scientific event or a spiritual experience depends on planning and preparation. If someone desires serenity and dignity, with control over the setting and treatments, those decisions must be made while conscious and competent. Otherwise, the status quo medical approach engulfs, sweeping up the sick, frail, and injured. Ultimately, life *will* end, although medicine may postpone that eventuality. However much we try to repress, dismiss, or deny the specter of terminality, our common fate finds us, distinguished by cause and date and possibly the suffering that precedes the last breath. Living fully and dying well require dropping the pretense and facing facts, exploring protocols, and preparing before receiving a fatal diagnosis or experiencing debilitating symptoms.

Share: To live wholeheartedly requires courage and action: having Advance Directives completed and retrievable and naming a health care agent who knows your wishes. Who do you trust to make decisions about your life? Designate your surrogates. Document your desires. Discuss with those who need to know. This is your life. Empower people who are willing to honor your wishes, not insistent on imposing their beliefs on you.

Care: Love is the bottom line. Loving means losing. It's part of being human, although we'd prefer to skip the pain. Love can help us overcome the emotions that hold us back: fear, inertia, and denial. Love is a feeling, but it's also about making choices and taking action. As you gather your treasures and prepare a map, imagine this as your last, best gift – a good goodbye for those you have loved most.

Acknowledging that human beings have mental, emotional, and spiritual facets in addition to physicality allows us to face and transcend humanity's primal existential crisis – the seeming finality of death. Life's magnum opus – the masterpiece – is not the physical body, which fails and dies, but the body of work, service, and love that prevail. How will we be remembered? How will we touch future generations? If we acknowledge death and admit life doesn't last, it can jolt us awake. Dying and its aftermath will not be easy. But with the right mindset and proactive preparation, it can be transformative and empowering and provide opportunities for healing and restoration. There is no single route for dying well, but unless planning takes place before needed, the medicalized body-fixation default will triumph and death becomes an ending without redemption.

Beings who live long enough are susceptible to aging and death. We will make acquaintance with illness, impairment, or injury. But even when a cure is impossible, we can hope for healing. Knowing that we get closer to the end every day, we can choose to be Aware, be Prepared, and Share. Along the way, we will share love, learn lessons, bring light, and leave a legacy. Let us live a life of purpose, prepare for the end, and ensure that the things that matter most will prevail. We can live fully, deeply, and humbly, even knowing that life begets death. The end of life will usher in grief, but it doesn't have to create chaos. Before the spark fades, marshal your courage and resources to face the existential dilemma of transience. If you're reading this, you still have time to face the reality and avoid painful consequences.

Everything comes to an end, including *Good Goodbyes*. My hope is that this book may help guide you on the path back to Mystery. Thanks for letting me walk with you. Don't forget to say goodbye before you go.

> Our days may come to seventy years, or eighty…
> they quickly pass, and we fly away.[88]

EPILOGUE

∞

HAPPILY EVER AFTER – DOESN'T HAPPEN BY CHANCE

Choice or chance? Can we take action or will we be forced to change? Are you willing to commit to taking steps to improve and advocate for intentional end-of-life experiences for yourself and loved ones?

1. Awaken to the journey. Be grateful for the gift of time. Celebrate, if you happen to win the genetic and social lottery.[89] "Don't cry because it's over. Smile because it happened."[90]

2. Face impermanence. Loss is the price we pay for living. Balance carpe diem with *set it and forget it* plans for the "Dead End" eventuality.

3. Examine your values. What makes your heart sing?[91] Feeling

alive is more about vitality than vital signs. If you follow a faith tradition, investigate what your religion actually teaches about end-of-life.[92]

4. Consider your legacy. Invest in growth – health, connections, and education.

5. Fix the roof while the sun is shining. There may not be a cloud on the horizon, but life can change in a blink. Be prepared. Plan for contingencies.

6. Carry an ICE-card (in case of emergency) indicating your next of kin and a summary of your medical history.

7. If you live alone or with a companion animal, consider how someone would get notified and have access to your home to care for you or your pet in an emergency.

8. Consider who you trust with your life. Most Advance Directives are vaguely written. Your surrogate, whether identified by you or by law, will be asked to make life-and-death decisions. If your preferences matter, choose ahead of time and talk to that person about your values and desires.

9. Make peace. You never know when a kiss will be the last. If you love someone and/or someone loves you, prepare for death realistically, practically, and emotionally. Imagine it as a post-dated love letter that shows you care.

10. Make sure your Advance Directive is retrievable. Upload it to a cloud-based repository so it's available and accessible at the moment of need.

11. May we recognize all that is unlived in us while we can still do something about it. What's on your bucket list?

12. Let go. Go forth to love and to serve. May your living and dying be fruitful.

APPENDICES

Appendix 1. Treasure Map

VERY IMPORTANT People & Papers (VIPS)

- ○ When needed, contact the Survivor Assistance Team @ _____
- ○ Treasure Chest location: _____
- ○ List updated: _____

	Essential Helpers	Names:	Date:	Discussed
☐	Health Care Proxy			☐
☐	Durable Power of Attorney (POA)			☐
☐	Executor/Personal Representative			☐

	Essential Papers	Place (Documents Location)	Updated:	Complete
ICE	In Case of Emergency (ICE) card	Wallet		☐
Med	Medical Directives / Living Will (includes Health Care Proxy)	Treasure Chest: Paper copy / Cloud: link to digital document		☐
VIPs	Very Important People (immediate critical notifications)	Treasure Chest list: Family members, Funeral home, minister, executor		☐
VIPs	Very Important Papers list	Treasure Chest		☐
Death	Funeral arrangements	Treasure Chest		☐
Death	Obituary	Treasure Chest: Draft copy on USB drive		☐
Legal	Will	Treasure Chest: Original in Locked box		☐
Legal	Durable Power of Attorney (POA)	Treasure Chest		☐
Legal	Trust	Treasure Chest (if applicable)		☐
Money	Passwords	Treasure Chest: paper & digital copies		☐
Money	Financial account information	Treasure Chest: paper & digital copies		☐
House	House operating procedures & keys	Treasure Chest		☐
Money	Wallet inventory	Treasure Chest		☐
Money	Safe deposit box bank & key	Treasure Chest (if applicable)		☐
Stuff	Inventory of household items	Treasure Chest: document on USB drive		☐
Stuff	Personal Property Disposition (PPD)	Treasure Chest: Who gets what		☐

	Helpers	Document	Names:	Contact info:	Informed
☐	Accountant	VIP list			☐
☐	Financial Planner	VIP list			☐
☐	Lawyer	VIP list			☐
☐	Guardian (children)	See Will			☐
☐	Owner (for pets)	See PPD			☐

VIP notifications following a loved one's death:

- ☐ Funeral Home
- ☐ Alumni organizations
- ☐ Banks, financial institutions
- ☐ Credit agencies
- ☐ Financial advisers, stockbrokers
- ☐ Insurance companies
- ☐ Military: Defense Finance and Accounting Services (DFAS) www.dfas.mil & Department of Veterans Affairs (VA)
- ☐ Social Security Administration
- ☐ ARMY & AIR FORCE MUTUAL AID ASSN (AAFMAA) AT WWW.AAFMAA.ORG FOR THOSE WITH AAFMAA INSURANCE

A downloadable version of this chart is available at www.opusonestudios.com

Appendix 2.
Military Resources

"Thank you for your service"
On Behalf of a Grateful Nation ..

Joan Grey, US Army (RET)

Walking to the Administration Building at Arlington National Cemetery (ANC) before a funeral, I pass Private First Class (PFC) Albert Gallo's gravestone (Section 54, Grave 5539-1). His marker gives a surprising amount of information. PFC Gallo (1924 – 2013) lived to age 89, served in World War II, was a Prisoner of War (POW), and was awarded the Purple Heart. My online search didn't find any further information. I don't even know whether he served in the Pacific or European theater or the circumstances of his POW experience.

Whereas most gravestones at Arlington have a religious symbol like a cross, this grave has an Infinity sign, which represents eternity and recognizes the paradox: We're NOT going to live forever, but part of us is perpetual. The marker also differs from many graves at ANC by including a quote: "With malice toward none," a line from President Lincoln's Second Inaugural Address. From the brief information on his stone, we know this about PFC Gallo: he was wounded in action, was captured by an enemy, and imprisoned as a POW. And yet judging from the inscription despite his trauma, PFC

Gallo's parting gift was an appeal for reconciliation, a message of mercy and forgiveness.

Life is not only measured by the years we live, but by what we do with those years. The carvings on a gravestone represent a distillation of the essence of a person. Legacy is how you live, how you die, and what you leave behind. Have you given any thought to how you want to be remembered? Will your final resting place include a grace note for the ages?

You served. Maybe for a single enlistment or possibly for much of your adult life. Whether you were drafted or volunteered, the United States of America recognizes your sacrifices and says "Thank you for your service" by providing some tangible benefits. These don't come automatically, so you need to plan ahead and instruct your survivors on what to ask for. In addition to checklists provided throughout *Good Goodbyes,* this section identifies military-specific entitlements.

The military doesn't conduct an operation without thorough

contingency planning. So, consider this your Warning Order for End of Life—plan for tomorrow today. Dying is a path we will all eventually take, prepared or not. The more work you do in advance, the easier it will be for your loved ones. Do you remember this saying from your time in the military: Proper Prior Planning Prevents Piss Poor Performance? A possible corollary adage for your legacy planning: Dealing with Death and Defining your Destiny is your Duty to your Descendants.[93]

During a time of great stress, families need direction and information, instead of the prospect of a scavenger hunt, where they end up scrambling to find information and put together the necessary paperwork. Since you won't have a sergeant telling you what to do and when to do it, planning is up to you. Make sure your *In Case of Emergency* (ICE) documents are easy-to-access and straightforward, rather than compounding a crisis with uncertainty. Keep in mind: planning ahead is an ultimate act of love.

Planning Pays Off

My last assignment in the Army was as a paratrooper at Fort Bragg. Airborne operations are inherently high-risk; a safe airdrop takes meticulous preparation. With a drop height of 1250 feet, time in the air from aircraft door to ground goes quickly. Much of what goes into a mass-tactical parachute operation takes place behind the scenes, before a soldier launches into the sky.

Planning, preparation, and training are vital to the mission success of any military maneuver. The same could be said about the work you do before your D-Day (Destiny Day). Everyone is eventually a *short timer*, closing in on ETS: "expiration – term of service." A service member's contract expires on a known ETS date. But a lot of planning and decision-making take place before that time: whether to leave the military or to re-up with a new enlistment contract.

Life also has an ETS, an expiration date when our earthly term of service ends. Unlike a service member's ETS date, our life expiration date is not so definitive: it's not spelled out in a contract and there's no fortune-telling app or crystal ball that clues you in. That means each of us has to be in ready mode, because we don't always know when we'll alerted for emergency muster to grab our gear and go.

We know in the abstract that life will end. But accepting the reality is different. The intensity and immediacy of bad news, such as learning that you have a terminal illness or being notified about a loved one's death can feel overwhelming, unsettling, and devastating. Advance planning can ease the stress of a difficult time. Being ready and knowing what to do ahead of time can allow survivors to focus on grieving and dealing emotionally with the loss, rather than trying to figure out whether they can afford to pay for a funeral or to stay in their house. Taking care of your loved ones pays dividends: peace of mind for you and the burden eased for your survivors.

There are certain things about life you can't change, so work on what you can control. Don't walk into a predictable ambush. Let your loved ones know. Have a plan. Collect your papers. Give survivors a checklist outlining steps to take, who to call, and where documents are located. Just like with military maneuvers – you often get only one chance to get it right. Do the planning to reduce the turmoil.

Before mobilization or deployment, the military requires Soldier Readiness Processing (SRP), a program to ensure that individuals are administratively, financially, legally, logistically, medically, and spiritually ready for their upcoming assignment. The military understands that soldiers and families need to have hard discussions before deploying. In life, there's no drill sergeant who makes sure that you and your family have your act together for whatever the future holds. It's up to you to initiate the process and discuss Wills, powers of attorney, and finances with anyone who loves you and would worry about you. Make sure family members have the information they need during your temporary or permanent absence. You might consider this work as your Life Readiness Process (LRP), because you never know…

Practicalities of Process (Partner, Chest, Map)

The work of being ready for whatever life might throw your way is important, but it's usually not urgent. Many consider the topic scary and the work tedious, which makes it easy to ignore or put off. Here are ideas for smoothing, and perhaps hurrying the process:

1. **Choose a buddy:** An accountability partner can help motivate you to work through the process and complete the steps.

2. **Find a container:** Identify a treasure chest. Pick something that suits your style, whether it's a box, a binder, or an expandable file folder. Take the time to find a home (physical and digital) for storing important documents and tangible assets.

3. **Leave a map:** Like pirates who draw a map to help find buried loot, reveal the location of your treasures. If you've done the work, ensure it pays off. Let your loved ones know your wishes and that they can find your "treasures," whether documents, jewelry, or the location of a storage unit or safe deposit box. Talk about it. Once is probably not enough.

And finally, remember timing is everything. You don't know how much advance warning you'll get. Have your "go-bag" packed and be ready to head out the door.

Helpers:

During the legacy planning process, who will keep you on track and suggest course adjustments where necessary?

We want to make sure that our families are taken care of, not only now, but in the future when we're not around. Being proactive can smooth the path for survivors and ensure they will receive all benefits they're entitled to because of your service. Actions you can take now include making a list of contacts, explaining the sequencing of notifications, and collecting essential documents. Does it sound like a lot of work? It is. The military benefits process is complicated and time sensitive. And most people don't have experience with it, until they're in the midst of a crisis.

Thankfully, there are navigators who are familiar with the steps and available to serve as guides for survivors. For critically injured or deceased service members, the military will assign a Casualty Assistance Officer (CAO) to assist the next-of-kin. Casualty assistance is an additional duty, based on a "duty roster," rather than being someone's primary job. While most CAOs work hard, they must learn policies and procedures to ensure that families get the support that they need, such as counseling on available benefits, facilitating payment of gratuities, and preparing for military honors. Additionally, since CAOs are assigned from military bases, they are primarily available for active-duty deaths, rather than for retirees or veterans, especially if the death occurs at a distance from a military base. General Officers are an exception; they will get an assigned liaison.

One organization includes providing assistance for military survivors as part of its mission. American Armed Forces Mutual Aid Association (AAFMAA), a not-for-profit organization serving the US military since

1879, can make the claims process easier and will assist military families wherever they are located. One benefit included with the purchase of an AAFMAA Life Insurance policy or a standalone policy is access to a Survivor Assistance Team, to guide next-of-kin in the aftermath of death. An AAFMAA representative, who works exclusively on survivor assistance, will offer personalized one-on-one service to AAFMAA members. Member spouses receive reciprocal benefits. AAFMAA is a one-stop-survivor-shop specializing in all aspects of military entitlements, including VA benefits, Survivor Benefit Plan (SBP), Social Security, Medicare, TRICARE for Life, and Federal Civilian Benefits. If a beneficiary passes away, AAFMAA will assist in filing claims with insurance companies as well as notifying government agencies to stop SBP premiums and VA payments. It will also update beneficiary forms for those agencies and life insurance policies.

Death will be a time of emotional upheaval and a substantial administrative burden, involving dozens of pages of forms to complete. AAFMAA tries to make it as easy as possible for member families at their time of need. When you're out of the picture, an AAFMAA team member steps in to explain the process, notify government agencies, and ensure that all eligible benefits and entitlements are applied for. Don't make your survivors navigate the maze of government bureaucracies without a guide at the side.

A family can get AAFMAA's Standalone Survivor Assistance Services after a servicemember dies, especially for help with filing a complex claim for VA benefits. However, the best time is ahead of time, so a member can locate and upload all of the important papers (DD 214, marriage certificate, VA disability paperwork, Social Security cards, etc.). Then when the AAFMAA member dies, one phone call to AAFMAA will initiate the survivor claims process.

Be proactive. Don't wait for a calamity to happen. Locate and upload your essential documents to AAFMAA's digital and physical vaults for document safekeeping, to expedite receiving military benefits, and to allow for ease of access from anywhere in the world.

Money:

Take these steps ahead of time in order to facilitate your family's access to monetary benefits.

Military retired pay: Military retired pay stops at death. The pay deposited for the month in which a veteran's death occurs will be recovered by DFAS (Defense Finance Accounting Service). After audit, a prorated amount will be paid to the beneficiary. Expect this process to take several months to complete. Adjustments will be initiated after receipt of a copy of the veteran's death certificate.

Survivor Benefit Plan (SBP): Because a servicemember's retirement benefits terminate upon death, the Survivor Benefit Plan (SBP) lets a retiree ensure his/her dependents receive an after-death annuity. SBP is based on a percentage of a service member's retired pay (maximum of 55%). At retirement from the military, a servicemember must opt into the system and pay premiums in order to obtain after-death SBP coverage for a designated beneficiary. Refer to your retiree pay statement to review your SBP coverage information.

Veteran's Administration Benefits:

Veteran's compensation: If servicemember was getting VA benefits, the surviving spouse is entitled to receive the benefit for the month in which s/he died.

Burial stipend: The VA provides some financial help to an eligible survivor to offset the cost of a veteran's funeral. A one-time burial allowance for a non-service-connected death is $300, and $2,000 for a military service-connected death. https://www.va.gov/burials-memorials/veterans-burial-allowance/

Service-connected death stipend: If the veteran's death is a result of the service-connected disability or a presumptive disease, a veteran's survivor may be eligible for additional benefits from the VA. Be aware: The cause of death on the death certificate must match the veteran's service-connected disability. A surviving spouse is sometimes eligible for Dependency and Indemnity Compensation (DIC), a non-taxable monthly payment. Receiving DIC may reduce the amount of the SBP annuity.

Final Resting Places

One of the Arlington Ladies I worked with would visit her husband's burial spot each time she was in the cemetery. She called her deceased husband's grave – her "forever home" – knowing that she will join him there one day.

Burial benefits through the VA include a gravesite in any national cemetery with available space, opening and closing of the grave, perpetual care, a government headstone or marker, a burial flag, and a Presidential Memorial Certificate at no cost to the family. Alternatively, the government can provide no-cost headstones for veterans at most private cemeteries.

Military Honors: On Behalf of a Grateful Nation

"In life, s/he honored the flag.
In death, the flag will honor him [or her]."
Chaplain's words before the flag folding at
Arlington National Cemetery graveside services.

If you've attended a military funeral, you're aware of how moving, solemn, and respectful they are. Rendering honors demonstrates the nation's gratitude to those who have defended our country. Paying final ceremonial respect recognizes the contributions and sacrifices of those who have served in the military. Each ceremony follows a standard sequence of events.

- Pallbearers from the honor guard carry the coffin or cremains.
- Optional: At the family's request, and if available, a chaplain will perform a graveside service.
- A firing party fires three volleys. The three-volley salute has historical significance. On the battlefield, warring sides would cease hostilities until the firing of three volleys, which indicated that the dead had been properly cared for and signaled that the fight could resume. Three also represents the essence of military service: Duty, Honor, Country.
- A bugler plays Taps.
- The casket team folds the flag.
- The non-commissioned officer or officer in charge (NCOIC/OIC) presents the folded American flag to the next of kin. using a standardized speech: "On behalf of the President of the United States, the United States _____ [Army, Marine Corps, Navy, Air Force, OR Coast Guard] and a grateful nation, please accept

this flag as a symbol of our appreciation for your loved one's honorable and faithful service."

A funeral director can help the family request military funeral honors.

National VA Cemeteries

The Department of Veterans Affairs maintains 151 national cemeteries in 42 states and Puerto Rico. This total number is misleading; some cemeteries listed do not accept new burials. Over 100 cemeteries are closed to new internments or open for cremations only. Also, not every state has a VA national cemetery. Since the VA's website isn't particularly intuitive or user-friendly, rather than searching by zip code or state, visit the VA cemetery national link at https://www.cem.va.gov/cems/allnational.asp instead, which shows availability of burial space.

Arlington National Cemetery (ANC)

Eligibility: Arlington National Cemetery's eligibility requirements for burial and inurnment are different, and more stringent, than national cemeteries maintained by the Department of Veterans Affairs. Eligibility will be determined at the time of need. ANC's requirements are a moving target. For the current rules, check out this fact sheet: https://www.arlingtoncemetery.mil/Portals/0/ANC%20Eligibility%20Fact%20Sheet%2004-03-2019.pdf

Arlington National Cemetery renders three levels of burial honors: military funeral honors, military funeral honors with escort, and dependent honors. Every uniformed service member or veteran of the armed forces is eligible for military funeral honors provided by the decedent's branch of service. https://www.arlingtoncemetery.mil/Funerals/About-Funerals/Military-Honors

Scheduling a funeral at ANC: Upon the death of the veteran or veteran's spouse, the primary next of kin (PNOK) or person authorized to direct disposition (PADD) should contact a funeral home to arrange for any desired services. The PNOK, PADD or the funeral director should call Arlington National Cemetery's customer service center at 1-877-907-8585 to arrange for the interment/inurnment service.

Be aware—it can take 6-8 months from the time for death for the service to take place. Several friends whose husbands have been awaiting burial have been distressed by a seeming lack of updates provided by the ANC scheduling department. One friend was informed by the cemetery representative a half hour before the burial service that she had to modify the gravestone inscription she requested and provide it by the next day.

VA Cemetery Pre-Qualification:

The Veterans' Administration offers a pre-need determination to confirm eligibility for burial in a VA National Cemetery prior to the veteran's death. Submit VA Form 40-10007 to receive this determination. An online-fillable copy of the Pre-Need Determination of Eligibility for Burial in a VA National Cemetery is available. https://www.va.gov/find-forms/about-form-40-10007/ For more information, check out the VA National Cemetery Administration website https://www.cem.va.gov/.

PLEASE NOTE: The VA Pre-Need Determination does NOT work

for all cemeteries, such as Arlington National Cemetery or the United States Soldiers and Airmen's Home National Cemetery. The Department of the Army, not the VA, has jurisdiction over those cemeteries.

State Veterans Cemeteries

Many states have established veterans' cemeteries, which are solely state-run. Eligibility is similar to that of VA national cemeteries, but may include residency requirements. Contact a specific cemetery for information. https://www.cem.va.gov/cems/listcem.asp

Grave Locator:

- Arlington National Cemetery's app (ANC Explorer) enables families, visitors and the public to locate gravesites, events or other points of interest throughout the cemetery. It allows viewing a photo of a headstone's front and back sides and getting directions to a particular location. Download the free app to your mobile device using the Apple Store or Google Play. Launch ANC Explorer from a desktop browser at https://www.arlingtoncemetery.mil/Explore/Find-a-Grave
- The Veterans Affairs (VA) provides information on service members buried in VA National Cemeteries.
- The American Battle Monuments Commission provides information on service members buried in overseas cemeteries.

Legacy: Hero's Story

When you're gone, make sure you're not forgotten. Before deployment, soldiers often write and leave behind a letter to be opened in case they don't return. In the event of tragedy, families appreciate messages as a reminder that love continues beyond space and time.

Another way to ensure your legacy lasts is through the stories you've left behind. The Veterans History Project (VHP) is a program of the Library of Congress American Folklife Center. It was established by Congress in 2000 with a mission "to collect, preserve, and make accessible the personal accounts of America's wartime Veterans so that future generations may hear directly from Veterans and better understand the realities of war." The program relies on interviews conducted according to defined guidelines by a network of volunteers including veteran service organizations, schools, healthcare providers, community groups, scout troops, and families.

To help facilitate the interview process, the Veterans History Project offers a Field Kit with instructions and the forms that participants will need to sign, the type of formatting the project requires for audio, video and photographs, and data sheets to help identify the materials being provided.

If you attended a military academy or belong to an alumni group, think about asking some friends to write your memorial article. (Yes, your friends may find the request strange...) Editors of West Point's yearbook, *Howitzer*, would ask Firsties (seniors) to have a classmate write the paragraph accompanying each graduate's photo. Let someone else prepare a draft and you can edit. As a Harley Davidson advertisement suggests: "When writing the story of your life, don't let anyone else hold the pen." Who will you trust to write something as important as your memorial article or obituary?

Last Words are Lasting Words:

Arlington National Cemetery is the final resting place for many heroes; PFC Gallo is just one. Like Gallo's memorial marker, the message carved on your gravestone will summarize your story for eternity. Consider this as your blank slate, your final creation. Do it ahead of time and imagine it as a vision board for how you want to live your remaining days and be remembered. How did you live; who did you love; what are you proud of; what are you leaving behind? Is there a quotation or verse that summarizes your life's philosophy?

Each day you're building the legacy that you'll leave behind. Until it's carved in stone, you can change. Plan ahead. https://www.va.gov/burials-memorials/memorial-items/headstones-markers-medallions/

Conclusion

In life, you honored the flag and cared for your family. The United States has tried to take care of you in death; ensure that your planning and preparation will honor and benefit your loved ones. When your time on earth is done, it's up to you; to pay it forward by ensuring your loved ones' well-being.

A secure future doesn't happen by chance. The important benefits earned through your service can be significant, but only if your loved ones know about their entitlements. In the midst of emotional trauma, figuring out how to claim those benefits can be overwhelming. The military will make efforts to provide the best possible support and care for families of deceased servicemembers, but they need your help. Get yourself squared away. Act now, to make it easier later. Collect the documents. Tell your family where to find things. Be Aware. Prepare. Share. Because you Care.

> And when our work is done,
> Our course on earth is run,
> May it be said, Well done.
> Be thou at peace.[94]

Planning Hints:

- **Don't wait.** Do it, before you need it.
- **Safety net:** Have financial reserves: don't make your loved one worry about whether s/he can afford to stay in your home. It can take months before a beneficiary starts receiving Survivor Benefits after filing the paperwork. In the meanwhile, you will have to count on your emergency funds.
- **Safeguard:** Keep important documents in a safe place.
- **Accessible:** Let your family know where your important papers are and how to access them.
- **Current:** Keep your personal and financial information up-to-date.

Essential Military-Specific Documents and Information

Gather the essential documents needed to file for military benefits and entitlements. Only one – your death certificate – will be issued at a later date. Collect the others and have them readily accessible. If you need to, request replacement copies of military records (e.g., DD214) ahead of time https://www.archives.gov/veterans/military-service-records/ standard-form-180.html#nok

- Veteran's name, social security number, and date of death
- Manner of death
- Marital status upon death
- If married: Name of spouse, social security number, address, date of birth, and date of marriage
- Marriage certificate or copies of birth certificates for dependent children
- Discharge from Active Duty (DD-214)
- Recent Leave & Earnings Statement (LES) or Retired Pay Statement
- VA disability award letters and rating decisions
- Death certificate (Date -- To Be Determined [TBD])

Resources:

Acronym	Organization	Website	Contact information
AAFMAA	American Armed Forces Mutual Aid Association	www.aafmaa.com	800-522-5221
ANC	Arlington National Cemetery	https://www.arlingtoncemetery.mil/ Funerals/Scheduling-a-Funeral	877-907-8585
Archives	National Archives and Records Administration	vetrecs.archives.gov	866-272-6272; Military records replacement copies (e.g., DD214); For veterans or next-of-kin of a deceased veteran
DEERS	Defense Enrollment Eligibility Reporting System	www.tricare.mil/DEERS	800-538-9552

DFAS	Defense Finance and Accounting Services	www.dfas.mil	800-321-1080
OPM	Office of Personnel Management	www.opm.gov	888-767-6738; government retirees
SSA	Social Security Administration	www.ssa.gov	800-772-1213
TRICARE	TRICARE healthcare system	www.tricare.mil	866-307-9749
USAFA	Air Force Academy	https://www.usafa.org/Heritage/ Notify_GraduateDeath	
USCGA	Coast Guard Academy	https://www.cgaalumni. org/s/1043/uscga/index. aspx?sid=1043&gid=1&pgid=2681	
USMA	West Point	https://www.westpointaog.org/ DettreMemorialProgram https://www.westpointaog.org/ westpointcemeteryeligibility https://www.westpointaog.org/ academyfuneralsupport	West Point cemetery Funeral Arrangements: 845.446.1620 memorialaffairs@ westpoint.edu memorial.support@ wpaog.org
USMMA	Merchant Marine Academy	https://www.usmmaalumni. com/s/1860/18/interior. aspx?sid=1860&gid=2&pgid=493	
USNA	Naval Academy	https://www.usna.com/memorial- affairs	410-295-4064
VA	Department of Veterans Affairs (VA)	www.va.gov	800-827-1000
VA	VA National Cemeteries	https://www.cem.va.gov/cems/ allnational.asp	Indicates whether a cemetery has available burial space

Reflections:

- Think of a Lazarus moment, whether a near-death you've experienced personally or when you've been with someone as they've been dying. What did you learn?
- Dying and death are hard topics for people to deal with. Have you made peace with your fears? How have you put good intentions into action?
- The "dash," the time between your birth and death dates, is more important than the beginning or ending. Are you happy with how you're living your "dash"?

Appendix 3.
Resources for Reflection
and Discussion

Movies: Use these movies to learn something new or see things in a new light…

- *50/50:* A man learns that he has malignant spinal tumors with a 50/50 chance of survival. The patient survives chemo and surgery, betrayal and expectations.
- *The Barbarian Invasions*: This French-Canadian film examines assisted suicide, the importance of restored relationships, and the meaning of a good ending. What constitutes a good goodbye and dignified death?
- *Beaches*: Two childhood friends are there for each other through life's ups and down – forever friends.
- *Breathe:* Based on a true story of a man with polio who lives a full life of invention, advocacy and adventure despite being paralyzed and requiring a respirator. The protagonist's physical restrictions led him to become a advocate for disability rights.
- *The Bucket List*: Before they "kick the bucket," two terminally ill men embark on a road trip with a wish list of things to see and do before they die. Despite differences, they want to come to terms with who they are and what life has meant. And so the adventure begins…
- *Christmas in August:* A terminally ill photographer and photo shop owner befriends a meter maid. Set in Seoul.
- *The Doctor*: A self-centered doctor's cancer diagnosis makes him better able to empathize with his patients and appreciate life.

- *Dying Young:* The professional relationship between a young man with cancer and his caretaker develops into a romance.
- *Get Low:* A hermit, avoided by many of his neighbors, decides to throw himself a party before he kicks the bucket.
- *Ikiru:* A old man with cancer vows to make his final days meaningful. Inspired by a co-worker, he adopts a project: he orchestrates building a playground in a slum. The park completion brings peace and acceptance. Bringing happiness to others brought a sense of purpose to his life.
- *I'll Be Me* features singer/songwriter Glen Campbell's farewell tour in the midst of his Alzheimer's diagnosis. It reveals how the family copes with the early stages of his dementia. The movie includes the last song Campbell wrote: "I'm Not Gonna Miss You."
- *Last Holiday:* How would you spend your last months if you were diagnosed with a terminal illness?
- *The Leisure Seeker:* Traveling in their recreational vehicle, a couple takes one last road trip before his Alzheimer's and her cancer can catch up with them.
- *Life as a House:* A man gets fired, has a breakdown, and learns he has terminal cancer. After diagnosis, he decides to take control by tackling a life-long goal: he tears down an old beach house and builds a new house, in the process reclaiming parts of himself and healing relationships.
- *My Life:* A man, whose wife is pregnant, is diagnosed with terminal cancer. The father-to-be makes a video diary, hoping to pass along wisdom to the child he will not live to meet.
- *Obit* (documentary) looks at the creation of newspaper obituaries. While the movie focuses on leaders and luminaries, the

writers' process gives insight into how we might shape the story of our lives.

- *Ordinary Love*: A middle-aged couple deals with a tough diagnosis
- *Other People*: A gay comedy writer returns home to take care of his dying mother, a family situation complicated by the staunch Catholic father's objections to his son's sexual orientation.
- *Stepmom:* shows a blended family dealing with the conflicts wrought by divorce and complicated by terminal diagnosis. The film portrays a broken family struggling for healing as death approaches.
- *Still Alice*: After troubling memory lapses, a professor is diagnosed with early onset Alzheimer's disease. Her children face the quandary of deciding whether to get tested to find out if they will develop the disease.
- *Terms of Endearment*: a woman with cancer overcomes relationship tensions to die surrounded by love: supported by her mother and reconciled with her ex-husband.
- *Wit*: Follows the illness and dying of a professor diagnosed with ovarian cancer. Portrays empathy and callousness of health care providers. Notable moment in the film: the CPR scene.
- Add your own: _____
- Add your own: _____
- Add your own: _____

Soundtracks:

- Alan Jackson – Remember When
- Ashley Campbell – Remembering
- Beatles – many

- Bee Gees – Too Much Heaven, Staying alive
- Beyoncé – XO (We don't have forever)
- Bon Jovi – It's My Life
- Brad Paisley – Last Time for Everything
- Bruce Springsteen – Dancing In the Dark
- Carly Simon – Anticipation
- Coldplay – Viva La Vida
- David Gates – Goodbye Girl
- David Gates & Bread – Everything I own
- Donna Taggart – Jealous Of The Angels
- Enya – Only Time
- Eric Clapton – Tears In Heaven
- Fleetwood Mac – Landslide
- Frozen – Let It Go
- Garth Brooks – If Tomorrow Never Comes, The Dance
- George Straight – Love Without End, Amen
- Gilbert O`Sullivan – Alone Again Naturally
- Glen Campbell – I'm Not Gonna Miss You
- Jim Croce – I'll Have To Say I Love You In A Song, Photographs and Memories
- John Lennon – Beautiful Boy, Watching the Wheels
- Kansas – Dust in the Wind
- Lady Gaga, Bradley Cooper – Shallow (from A Star Is Born)
- Lee Ann Womack – I Hope You Dance (In memory of Becky Blyth Hardy, 1957 -2021)
- Maroon 5 – Memories (In memory of Kevin Vance MacGibbon, 1958 - 2020)
- Mike + The Mechanics – The Living Years
- Norman Greenbaum – Spirit In The Sky

- Phil Collins – Can't Stop Loving You, Do You Remember, Everyday, One More Night, Since I Lost You, You'll Be in my heart
- Pink Floyd – Wish You Were Here
- R.E.M – Everybody Hurts [Look at subtitles on YouTube video: https://www.youtube.com/watch?v=5rOiW_xY-kc]
- Rita Wilson – Throw Me a Party
- Rolling Stones – Wild Horses
- Sarah McLachlan – In the Arms of an Angel, I Will Remember You
- Stevie Wonder – I Just Called to Say I Love You
- Wicked – For Good
- Wilson Phillips – Hold On
- Add your own: _____
- Add your own: _____
- Add your own: _____

Poetry and Books

- Amelia Josephine Burr, "A Song of Living"
- Author Unknown, "I Wrote Your Name"
- Author Unknown, "Not How Did He Die, But How Did He Live?"
- Author Unknown, "Prayer of Faith"
- Author Unknown, "Why"
- Christine Russo, "Lament for my unborn daughter"
- Dawna Markova, "I Will Not Die an Unlived Life"
- Edna St. Vincent Millay, "Dirge Without Music"
- Hafiz, "Blessing"
- Helen Steiner Rice, "No Night Without You"
- Henry Van Dyke, "For Katrina's Sun Dial"

- John Gillespie Magee, Jr, "High Flight"
- John Henry Newman, "Oh Lord, Support us all the day long," Book of Common Prayer
- John O'Donohue, "A Blessing for Death"
- John O'Donohue, "For the Dying"
- Judah Halevi, "Tis a Fearful Thing"
- Kahlil Gibran, "On Death"
- Laurence Binyon, "For the Fallen"
- Linda Ellis, "The Dash"
- Lisa Genova – fiction books with characters dealing with neurological disorders.
- Mary Lee Hall, "Turn Again to Life"
- Mary Oliver, "In Blackwater Woods"
- Merrit Malloy, "Epitaph"
- Rabbi Sylvan Kamens and Rabbi Jack Riemer, "A Litany of Remembrance"
- Rabindranath Tagore, "Peace My Heart"
- Rilke, "Go to the Limits of Your Longing"
- Rumi, "On the Day I Die"
- Rumi, "The Guest House"
- Sara Teasdale, "There Will Come Soft Rains"
- Sri Chinmoy, "Death is a Journey"
- Add your own: _____
- Add your own: _____
- Add your own: _____

Scripture – What Is Your Life Verse?

- Add your own: _____
- Add your own: _____
- Add your own: _____

Appendix 4.
Advance Planning Terms[95]

During *Good Goodbyes*, you've already considered what you'd want done or not done and who you'd want making decisions for you in the event of a medical emergency. Doctors may assume that you know what words and phrases in this glossary mean.

Advance Directives (AD): legal documents regulated by each state. 1. A **Living Will** provides instruction about a person's wishes for particular types of medical treatment. 2. A **health care power of attorney** identifies a person (also called surrogate, agent, or proxy) who can make decisions on behalf of another in the event of serious illness, incapacity, or inability to communicate. Using the principle of substituted judgment, doctors and family members try to make the decision that the patient would have made if he or she were able to speak and decide. If no document is prepared or can be found, the state will identify who is authorized to make decisions. Advanced directives augment other legal documents such as Wills or power of attorneys, which deal with property and financial affairs. Completion of Advance Directives is voluntary, but ALL adults should prepare and update these forms. Figure out how medical personnel will have access to your directives when needed.

Allow Natural Death (AND): a patient or proxy directs a doctor to withhold or withdraw life sustaining treatment in cases of terminal illness or permanent unconsciousness. It generally means no CPR or ventilator, but may also include refusing tube feeding and antibiotics in order to "let nature run its course." The underlying disease process is responsible for death; the interventions were prolonging dying. (The current US system defaults towards technological interventions. Natural death requires forethought, pre-planning, and documentation. Dignity and comfort have to be prearranged.)

Artificial Nutrition and Hydration (Tube Feeding): a clinical intervention for a patient who is unable to eat or drink through the mouth. Delivery methods to provide nutrients and fluids may include intravenous infusion of fluids (needle inserted in vein), a tube threaded into the nose for nasogastric feeding, or a surgically implanted PEG (percutaneous endoscopic gastrostomy). TPN (Total parenteral nutrition) is another term for a type of intravenous feeding.

Brain Death: irreversible loss of all brain functions. When the brain dies, the person is considered dead. There is a specific methodology for clinical assessment and confirmation before a brain death diagnosis is made. Brain death differs from persistent vegetative state, in which some autonomic functions remain.

Capacity: the insight and ability to understand a medical problem, comprehend the benefits and risks of treatment options, and to make decisions. An adult is assumed to have capacity unless it becomes clear that he/she cannot understand or evaluate information needed to decide or communicate wishes. Capacity differs from competency, which is a court–rendered legal determination.

Cardiopulmonary Resuscitation (CPR): a medical procedure done on a person whose heart has stopped (cardiac arrest) or breathing has stopped (respiratory arrest). It includes chest compressions and artificial ventilation. The patient may also receive electric shocks (defibrillation) and drugs.

Code: cardiac or respiratory arrest, when an individual stops breathing or his/her heart stops beating.

Competence: mental ability of a patient to participate in decision-making and be responsible for actions.

Do-Not-Resuscitate/Do Not Intubate (DNR/DNI): DNR and DNI are a doctor's written medical orders instructing the healthcare team not to attempt cardiopulmonary resuscitation (CPR) when the heart or breathing stops or to insert a tube to support breathing. The DNR/DNI is requested by a patient or family and must be ordered by a doctor to be valid. DNR may also be called a Comfort Care Order (CCO).

Double Effect: an ethical understanding that trying to relieve patient suffering through sedation may include the possible risk of depressing respiration and hastening death.

End of Life (EOL) (Terminal): patients are considered at the end-of-life when a doctor determines a person is likely to die within six months. This may include patients who have progressive incurable conditions like cancer or Alzheimer's; those with general frailty and co-existing conditions that mean they are expected to die; or those at risk of dying from a sudden acute crisis because of a pre-existing, life-threatening condition.

Healthcare Agent, Medical Surrogate: the person named in an advance directive or set by state law to make healthcare decisions for a person who is no longer able to make medical decisions for him/herself.

HIPAA—Health Insurance Portability and Accountability Act of 1996: legislation that safeguards the privacy of personal medical information.[96]

Hospice: care for terminally ill patients whose doctors have diagnosed six months of life remaining. Goals of care change from cure to comfort. This holistic approach combines medical care with pain management and emotional and spiritual support. Depending on where a person lives, care may be provided in the home (possibly a nursing home or assisted living facility) or a stand-alone inpatient hospice center. Medicare, Medicaid, and most private insurances cover hospice benefits.

In Case of Emergency (ICE): a document which provides emergency responders and hospital staff with the names and contact information for next-of-kin (NOK) contacts in case of medical emergency. It should also include a list of pre-existing conditions (like diabetes, hypertension, etc.) and a current list of medications. Some people setup an ICE contact in their phone, but if the device is password protected or breaks in an accident, the information is inaccessible.

Informed Consent: permissions granted by a patient to health care providers, who have provided an explanation of possible risks and benefits a suggested treatment entails and alternative interventions.

Intubation: insertion of a tube through the mouth or nose into the trachea (windpipe) to create and maintain an open airway to help the patient breathe. See ventilator.

Life Support: life-sustaining medical procedures that replace or support bodily functions. These may include CPR, breathing or feeding tubes, IVs, dialysis, or other treatments.

Living Will: form of advance directive in which a person indicates preferences about medical treatment if he or she is unable to communicate. It may also be called a "directive to physicians," "healthcare declaration," or "medical directive." This is usually paired with a Medical Power of Attorney.

Medical Power of Attorney: document that names someone for medical care decision-making in the event of incapacity. This form of advance directive also goes by the terms healthcare proxy, durable power of attorney for healthcare, or appointment of a healthcare agent. The person named may be called a healthcare agent, surrogate, attorney-in-fact, or proxy. See Advance Directives.

Natural Death: generally, an accidental occurrence in the US.

Next-of-Kin (NOK): a person's closest living blood relative or relatives. If a person has no documentation, each state has a defined priority for determination of NOK. Medical surrogate decision making laws allow a person to make decisions about medical treatments for a patient who is unable to make their own decisions and did not prepare an advance directive.

Organ Donation: providing an organ, eye, or tissue for the purpose of transplantation into another person. Donors can be living or dead. All major religions approve of organ and tissue donation. If a person or NOK agrees, doctors determine at the time of death who is eligible to donate what organs or tissues.

Palliative Care: holistic care of patients focused on managing pain as well as providing psychological, social, and spiritual support to patients and their family. Palliative care does not require a terminal diagnosis or life-limiting prognosis. The goal of palliative care is to provide the best quality of life available to the patient by relieving suffering and controlling pain and symptoms such as nausea, shortness of breath, anorexia, and fatigue.

Power of Attorney: legal document allowing one person to act in a legal matter on another's behalf about financial or real estate business.

Persistent Vegetative State (PVS): diagnosis when a patient has suffered brain trauma deemed irreversible, which is characterized by lack of consciousness and thought, is unresponsive to psychological and physical stimuli, and displays no sign of higher brain function. The person is kept alive only by medical intervention. Some reflex activities, such as breathing, blinking, or movements, may continue

Physician Order for Life-Sustaining Treatment (POLST): medical orders that detail specific medical treatments for individuals with a serious illness or advanced frailty near the end-of-life. POLST is a set of medical order whereas an Advance Directive provides general instructions from a person.

Patient Self-Determination Act (PSDA), 1990: most health care institutions (but not individual doctors) give patients a written summary of health care decision-making rights and the facility's policies regarding advance directives. It is the patient's responsibility to ensure your care team has a copy of the advance directive.

Ventilator, Respirator, Tracheotomy (AKA Vent or Trach): mechanical ventilator that forces air into the lungs through a tube that is inserted into the nose, mouth, or throat. The machine keeps oxygen moving through the patient's lungs. Because of discomfort, an intubated person requires sedation. If prolonged airway access is needed, doctors may perform a tracheostomy by cutting a hole in the throat to insert the breathing tube.

Voluntarily Stopping Eating and Drinking (VSED): a patient refuses food and liquids, including sustenance by feeding tube with the understanding this will hasten death. Former NPR radio host Diane Rehm talks about her husband's decision regarding VSED in her book *On My Own.*

Appendix 5.
12 Steps for Mortals

God, grant me the Serenity to
Accept the things I cannot change
Courage to change the things I can, and
Wisdom to know the difference.

We …

1. Admitted we are powerless over death. Morbidity curves can be flattened temporarily—only. Ultimately, mortality—stalking us since birth—wins. Our lives will be unmanageable until we face reality—life ends; all saves are temporary.

2. Came to believe that a power greater than ourselves could restore us to sanity and inspire us to plan and prepare for the final stage of life. We release our insanity—doing the same things repeatedly and expecting different results – in order to reclaim sanity.

3. Made a decision to turn our lives over to the care of a higher power, recognizing that medicine can provide only impermanent "saves." Health care workers are magician's assistants, not the Magician.

4. Made a fearless inventory of ourselves, including our false expectations and where we've missed the mark.

5. Admitted to a higher power, to ourselves, and to another human being the exact nature of our delusions.

6. Were entirely ready to have our higher power remove defects of character, including our obsessions with being alive, as a substitute for living fully. We also release our willingness to demonize the "other": those who think, look, or act differently.

7. Humbly asked our higher power to remove our shortcomings, including short-term thinking and what's-in-it-for-me (WIIFM) focus.

8. Made a list of all people we will harm if we don't change. Vowed to prepare advance directives, say the magic words (forgive me, I forgive you, thank you, I love you), and live a no-regrets life.

9. Made direct amends in a calm, non-judgmental voice to the people we love. Also, know there will be times we have unintentionally hurt others. Say you're sorry.

10. Continued to take personal inventory. When we were wrong, admitted it and tried to make amends: the next time, better.

11. Sought intentionally through prayer, meditation, and selfless actions to improve our conscious contact with our fellow beings, knowing that the spirit of the living God is present in each person. Recognizing that since God is not on social media, we "friend" the Divine by praying for insight of God's will for us and the power to carry that out (and not just make promises or talk about our good intentions).

12. Having had a spiritual / pragmatic / emotional / practical awakening as the result of these steps, we tried to carry this message to others, and to practice these principles in all our affairs.

AA's 12 Steps inspired me as I was writing *Good Goodbyes: A Mortal's Guide to Life*. *Good Goodbyes* presents a holistic approach for a universal problem. We can't solve death but we can ease its side effects by building a foundation for good goodbyes.

Appendix 6.
Consider Your Line in the Sand

Physical impairment
Personal Self-Assessment Scale (PSAS)[97]

						Personal Preferences			
PSAS Level	MOBILITY	ACTIVITY LEVEL & EVIDENCE OF DISEASE	SELF-CARE	INTAKE	CONSCIOUS LEVEL	DNR	No AN	No IVH	Other
PSAS 100%	Full	Normal activity & work No evidence of disease	Full	Normal	Full				
PSAS 90%	Full	Normal activity & work Some evidence of disease	Full	Normal	Full				
PSAS 80%	Full	Normal activity & work with effort Some evidence of disease	Full	Normal or reduced	Full				
PSAS 70%	Reduced	Unable normal activity & work Significant disease	Full	Normal or reduced	Full				
PSAS 60%	Reduced	Unable hobby/house work Significant disease	Occasional assistance	Normal or reduced	Full or confusion				
PSAS 50%	Mainly sit/lie	Unable to do any work Extensive disease	Considerable assistance	Normal or reduced	Full or drowsy or confusion				
PSAS 40%	Mainly in bed	Unable to do most activity Extensive disease	Mainly assistance	Normal or reduced	Full or drowsy +/- confusion				
PSAS 30%	Totally bed bound	Unable to do any activity Extensive disease	Total care	Reduced	Full or drowsy +/- confusion				
PSAS 20%	Totally bed bound	Unable to do any activity Extensive disease	Total care	Minimal sips	Full or drowsy +/- confusion				
PSAS 10%	Totally bed bound	Unable to do any activity Extensive disease	Total care	Mouth care only	Drowsy or coma				
PSAS 0%	Dead	-	-	-	-				

INSTRUCTIONS:

A) *Each PSAS level is explained by reading across the rows from left to right.*

B) After reviewing PSAS levels, move to the green columns under the title "Personal Preferences".

C) Each green "Personal Preference" column identifies medical decisions that you may choose in advance to have activated when you reach a certain PSAS level*:

DNR = *Do Not Resuscitate order (no CPR, electrical shocks, breathing tubes)*
No AN = *No artificial nutrition (example: feeding tubes)*
No IVH = *No IVs for artificial hydration*
Other = *Any medical treatment(s) that you may elect not to have (blood transfusions, dialysis, hospitalization for anything other than comfort care, etc). Details of the "Other" category must be listed in the space provided beneath the columns.*

D) For each medical decision that you wish to make in advance for yourself, place an "X" in each column (example, DNR) in the row matching the PSAS level of your choice (example, PSAS level 30%).

E) Sign and date this document. Place it in your living will. Give a copy to your health care provider, your surrogate medical decision maker and any family or friends whom you wish to have a copy. Take a copy with you whenever you go to see a doctor. You may write "**VOID**" on this document at any time, destroy it and create an updated version. Updated versions should be shared with your health care provider, your surrogate medical decision maker, and any family or friends who have a previous copy.

*** You must be fully conscious in order to make decisions for yourself in advance.**

Write your "Other" preferences here:

Sign your name: _____ Date: _____

Witness/Notary: _____ Date: _____

(It is strongly advised that this be reviewed at least every 6 months, or upon any major change in your medical condition in order to keep it current with your preferences. When renewing or if changes are needed, then use a new form with a new date of completion, and *destroy the older one.*)

Mental diminishment

Functional Assessment Staging Test

The Functional Assessment Staging Test (FAST) is the most well validated measure of the course of AD in the published, scientific literature.
The stages of Alzheimer's disease as defined by FAST are:

Stage	Stage Name	Characteristic	Expected Untreated AD Duration (months)	Mental Age (years)	MMSE (score)
1	Normal Aging	No deficits whatsoever	--	Adult	29-30
2	Possible Mild Cognitive Impairment	Subjective functional deficit	--		28-29
3	Mild Cognitive Impairment	Objective functional deficit interferes with a person's most complex tasks	84	12+	24-28
4	Mild Dementia	IADLs become affected, such as bill paying, cooking, cleaning, traveling	24	8-12	19-20
5	Moderate Dementia	Needs help selecting proper attire	18	5-7	15
6a	Moderately Severe Dementia	Needs help putting on clothes	4.8	5	9
6b	Moderately Severe Dementia	Needs help bathing	4.8	4	8
6c	Moderately Severe Dementia	Needs help toileting	4.8	4	5
6d	Moderately Severe Dementia	Urinary incontinence	3.6	3-4	3
6e	Moderately Severe Dementia	Fecal incontinence	9.6	2-3	1
7a	Severe Dementia	Speaks 5-6 words during day	12	1.25	0
7b	Severe Dementia	Speaks only 1 word clearly	18	1	0
7c	Severe Dementia	Can no longer walk	12	1	0
7d	Severe Dementia	Can no longer sit up	12	0.5-0.8	0
7e	Severe Dementia	Can no longer smile	18	0.2-0.4	0
7f	Severe Dementia	Can no longer hold up head	12+	0-0.2	0

Appendix 7.
Minimum Essentials for Young Families

You hope you'll never need a fire extinguisher, but many of us keep one in the kitchen, just in case.

Pilots hope that their plane will never crash in the water, but military aviators receive training and must demonstrate proficiency in aircraft ditching and underwater egress.

You hope you'll live long enough to see your children grow and launch, but life offers no guarantees.

Many find the topic of dying and death so unpleasant that it is easier to avoid than face. Just remember that it's likely that you'll grow old and be around long enough to annoy your kids. But hope is not a method and living during a global pandemic has only increased uncertainty. Parents should plan for the possibilities, while at the same time hoping you never need them.

You can probably think of a million things you'd rather do than tackle the difficult questions that surround contingency planning. We get it, but think about the alternative—a court has to step in to make decisions for your family. If something were to happen to you, steps you take today will contribute to your family's peace of mind and emotional and financial stability. Good intentions aren't enough. Life happens. In a crisis, you may not have the time, energy, or wherewithal to identify key people, prepare documents, and implement your plan. Having some medical, legal, and financial documents prepared is a way of taking care of your children.

No parent ever wants to imagine a day when they won't be there for their children. But what would happen if you became disabled or died? Have you considered who you would want as caretaker for your children? Would a guardian have sufficient resources to support a suddenly larger family? Would you want courts making decisions about your family's future? Three key areas to consider are medical, legal, and financial.

Medical: Who Will Make Medical Decisions If I'm Seriously Injured?

Many people think about estate planning in the context of death—but it's also important if you become sick or injured and are unable to make decisions for yourself. Every adult needs an advance directive that identifies a medical decision-maker and desired treatments. The medical directive (also called a Living Will) includes two parts: a durable power of attorney that gives a trusted person (also called an agent, proxy, or surrogate) the authority to make health care decisions if you can't. It also provides guidance on what medical treatments you might want. In case of an accident or sudden illness, this document will make things easier for your family and ensure someone can manage your care if you're not able to.

Legal: Who Will Take Care of My Children If Something Happens to Me?

Most people think about a Will as the document that distributes assets. But a Will also indicates a caretaker for minor children, if the need arises. Intentionally choosing a guardian protects your children and will alleviate stress and pain should you end up incapacitated. If parents die and have not chosen a guardian, a family court judge will make the selection. And parents will no longer be in a position to object if they are unhappy with the court-appointed guardian.

In picking a guardian, consider the following questions:

- Does this person share my values?
- Will this person provide the life I would want for my children?
- Does he/she have the parenting skills to provide a nurturing and safe environment?
- Is this person physically up to the task of raising children?
- Does this person have stable relationships and finances?

Imagining not being around to raise children is distressing, but even worse is not having a plan and subjecting children to uncertainty and stress in the aftermath of tragedy.

Financial: What Financial Safety Net Do I Have in Place?

You want financial security for your children, with some combination of amassing assets and acquiring insurance. Insurance policies that cover disability or death would replace earnings for a few years in case you can't work or in the event of an unexpected death. If you're reasonably young and healthy, term insurance, which stays in effect for a set number of years, is often a good choice for young parents. Also, decide who you want to have access to your assets and identify this person in a durable power of attorney. Authorizing a person ahead of time will eliminate the need for a court order.

Ensure your children have the financial security necessary to live their dreams, even if you're no longer around to directly support them. Your forethought will ease the way by providing funding to maintain your children's standard of living and provide future opportunities.

"Plan for the worst, hope for the best." Keep In Mind the Bottom Line Question—How Can I Make It Easier for Others?

Even if you don't have wealth, estate planning is valuable.

Even if you're young and healthy, you still need these documents. Young people can end up living a long time with catastrophic injuries. Having medical, legal, and financial documents will put you in the driver's seat and help minimize stress and confusion at a tumultuous time. Spelling out what you want to happen in a crisis, reduces the likelihood that disputes will arise. While they may never be used, if you became seriously ill or were injured, these documents let your family know what you would want, spare them difficult decisions, and preclude disagreements. Once your plan is in place, it's a good idea to review and update it periodically, especially after a major life event.

Pilots anticipate and train for things that might go wrong. They want to have practiced escape maneuvers ahead of time in a controlled setting, knowing that this will improve their prospect of surviving and thriving in the aftermath of a crash. Parents should bring that same better-safe-than-sorry attitude and level of preparation in order to ensure their family's future is bright, no matter what the circumstances.

This appendix contributed by Steven and Emily Grey

REFERENCES

Albom, Mitch. *Tuesdays with Morrie: an Old Man, a Young Man, and Life's Greatest Lesson.* 1st ed., Doubleday, 1997.

Becker, Ernest. *The Denial of Death.* New York: The Free Press, 1973.

Boyle, Patricia A., et al. "Effect of Purpose in Life on the Relation Between Alzheimer Disease.

Butler, Katy. *Knocking on Heaven's Door: The Path to a Better Way of Death.* New York: First Scribner, 2013. Print.

Byock, Ira. *The Best Care Possible: A Physician's Quest to Transform Care Through the End-of-life.* NY: Penguin Group, 2012.

Covey, Stephen R. *The Seven Habits of Highly Effective People: Restoring the Character Ethic.* Simon and Schuster, 1989.

Danticat, Edwidge. *The Art of Death: Writing the Final Story.* Graywolf Press, 2017.

---. "The Mysterious Power of Near-Death Experiences." *The New Yorker,* 2017.

---. *Untwine: A Novel.* NY: Scholastic, Inc., 2015.

Dunn, Hank. *Hard Choices for Loving People: CPR, Artificial Feeding, Comfort Care, and the Patient with a Life-Threatening Illness.* A & A Publishers, Incorporated, 2013.

Ehrenreich, Barbara. *Natural Causes: an Epidemic of Wellness, the Certainty of Dying, and Killing Ourselves to Live Longer.* New York: Twelve, 2018.

Emanuel, Ezekiel J, & Emanuel, Linda L. (1998). The promise of a good death. *Lancet,* 351, 21-29.

Fitzpatrick, Jeanne. *A better way of dying: how to make the best choices at the end-of-life.* Penguin Books, 2010.

Frankl, Viktor E. *Man's Search for Meaning.* New York: Pocket Books, 1984. Print.

Freed, Rachael. *Women's Lives, Women's Legacies: Creating Your Own Ethical Will,* 2nd ed.. Minneapolis: MinervaPress, 2012.

Gawande, Atul. *Being Mortal: Medicine and what Matters in the End.* New York: Metropolitan Books/Henry Holt and Company, 2014. Print.

---. Letting Go: What should medicine do when it can't save your life? *The New Yorker.* August 2, 2010. Online.

---. "The Way We Age Now: Medicine has increased the ranks of the elderly. Can it make old age any easier?" *The New Yorker.* April 30, 2007. Online.

Genova, Lisa. *Left Neglected*: a Novel. 1st Gallery Books hardcover ed., Gallery Books, 2011.

Gilbert, Daniel T., and Timothy D. Wilson. "Prospection: Experiencing the Future." *Science (New York,*

Halifax, Joan. *Being with Dying: Cultivating Compassion and Fearlessness in the Presence of Death.* Shambhala Publishers, 2009.

Harrington, Samuel. *At Peace: Choosing a Good Death after a Long Life.* NY: Hachette Book Group, 2018.

Hebb, Michael. *Let's Talk about Death (over Dinner): An Invitation and Guide to Life's Most Important Conversation.* Da Capo Press, Incorporated, 2018.

Hitchens, Christopher. *Mortality.* Atlantic, 2012.

Hoffner, Erik. "As We Lay Dying: Stephen Jenkinson On How We Deny Our Mortality." The Sun, August 2015. Print.

Holland, Jimmie, and Sheldon Lewis. *Human Side of Cancer.* 2009. Print.

Hollis, Jennifer L. *Music at the End-of-life: Easing the Pain and Preparing the Passage.* Religion, Health, and Healing. Santa Barbara, Calif.: Praeger, 2010.

Holy Bible, New International Version®, NIV®, 2011. Online. 2008.

Hopkins, Jeffrey. *Advice on Dying and Living a Better Life.* Atria Books, 2002.

Horn, Dara. *Eternal Life: a Novel.* First ed., W. W. Norton &Amp; Company, Inc., 2018.

Jennings, Dana. "10 Lessons of Prostate Cancer." *The New York Times* "Well Blog" Nov 25, 2008.

Kagan, Shelly. *Death*. Yale University Press, 2012.

Kalanithi, Paul. *When Breath Becomes Air*. Ed. A. (Abraham) Verghese. First edition. ed. New York: Random House, 2016. Print.

Kleinman, Arthur. "The art of medicine: Catastrophe and caregiving: the failure of medicine as an art." Lancet 371, no. 9606 (2008): 22-23.

Kleinman, Arthur, Leon Eisenberg, and Byron Good. "Culture, illness, and care: clinical lessons from anthropologic and cross-cultural research." Annals of Internal Medicine 88, no. 2 (1978): 251-258.

Kleinman, Arthur. *The Illness Narratives: Suffering, Healing, and the Human Condition*. New York: Basic Books, 1988.

Kübler-Ross, Elisabeth and David Kessler. *Life Lessons: Two Experts on Death and Dying Teach Us about the Mysteries of Life and Living*. Scribner, 2000.

Liu, Cixin. *The Three-Body Problem*. Ed. Ken Liu. New York: Tor, 2014. Print.

Lunney JR, Lynn J, Foley D, et al; Patterns of Functional Decline at the End-of-life. JAMA. 2003;289(18): 2387-2392. https://www.mypcnow.org/copy-of-fast-fact-325

Lynn, Joanne, et al. *Handbook for Mortals: Guidance for People Facing Serious Illness*. Oxford University Press, 1999.

Mannix, Kathryn. *With the End in Mind: Dying, Death and Wisdom in an Age of Denial*. Little, Brown and Company/Hachette Book Group, 2018.

McCorkle, Jill. "It's a funeral. RSVP." *Final Vinyl Days and Other Stories.* Algonquin Books of Chapel Hill, 1998.

Milligan, Stuart. "Addressing the Spiritual Care Needs of People near the End-of-life. (Learning Zone: End-of-life Care)(Cover Story)." *Nursing Standard* 26, no. 4 (2011): 47–56.

Mukherjee, Siddhartha. *The Emperor of All Maladies: A Biography of Cancer.* New York: Scribner, 2011.

Muller, Wayne. *How, Then, Shall We Live?: Four Simple Questions That Reveal the Beauty and Meaning of Our Lives.* Bantam Books, 1996.

Munson, Ronald, and Ian Lague. *Intervention and Reflection: Basic Issues in Bioethics.* Tenth edition. ed. Boston, MA: 2017. Print

Myers, Jo. Good to Go: *A Guide to Preparing for the End-of-life.* New York: Sterling Publishing, 2010.

Name Withheld By Request. "It's Over, Debbie." *JAMA* 259.2 (1988): 272. Print.

Narrative and Stories in Health Care: Illness, Dying, and Bereavement. Oxford ; New York: Oxford University Press, 2009.

Neumann, Ann. *The Good Death: an Exploration of Dying in America.* Beacon Press, 2016.

Nuland, Sherwin B. *How We Die: Reflections on Life's Final Chapter.* 1st ed. New York: Knopf, 1994. Print.

Paley Ellison, Koshin [editor]. *Awake at the Bedside: Contemplative Teachings on Palliative and End-of-Life Care.* Somerville, MA: Wisdom, 2016.

Paulson, Carole. "Educating for Mindful Perspectives on Aging." *The Journal of Nursing Education* 51, no. 6 (2012): 303–4. https://doi.org/10.3928/01484834-20120522-01.

Pearlman, Robert, et. al. *Your Life, Your Choices.* http://www.elderguru.com/downloads/your_life_your_choices_advance_directives.pdf

Peck, M. Scott. *The Road Less Traveled and beyond: Spiritual Growth in an Age of Anxiety.* Simon & Schuster, 1997.

Pollack, Harold. "Atul Gawande explains why the health care system should stop trying to help everyone live longer." *The Washington Post.* October 30, 2014. Online.

Pollan, Michael. *How to Change Your Mind: What the New Science of Psychedelics Teaches Us about Consciousness, Dying, Addiction, Depression, and Transcendence.* Penguin Press, 2018.

Qi, Jenny. *The Atlantic.* "My Mother Deserved to Die Comfortably." 6 Nov 2013.

Quill, Timothy E. *A Midwife through the Dying Process: Stories of Healing and Hard Choices at the End-of-life* . Baltimore: Johns Hopkins University Press, 1996.

Riggs, Nina. *The Bright Hour: A Memoir of Living and Dying.* New York: Simon & Schuster, 2017. Print.

Roach, Mary. *Stiff: the Curious Lives of Human Cadavers.* W.W. Norton & Co., 2003.

Rosenthal, Elisabeth. *An American Sickness: How Healthcare Became Big Business and How You Can Take It Back.* Penguin Press, 2017.

Schaper, Donna. *Approaching the End-of-life: a Practical and Spiritual Guide*. 2015.

Schneiderman, Lawrence. *Embracing Our Mortality: Hard Choices in an Age of Medical Miracles*. Oxford University Press, 2008.

Schwalbe, Will. *Books for Living*. First ed., Alfred A. Knopf, 2017.

Shneidman, Edwin. "Criteria for a Good Death." *Suicide and Life-Threatening Behavior*, vol. 37, no. 3, 2007, pp. 245–247.

Seneca, Letter 4, to Lucilis, "On the Terrors of Death."

Shelley, Mary Wollstonecraft. *Frankenstein, or, The Modern Prometheus*: Revised, Corrected, and Illustrated with a New Introduction, by the Author. Chadwyck-Healey, 1999.

Silverstein, Jason. Dying Well, SSCI E-121 Lecture slides.

Singh, Kathleen Dowling. *The Grace in Dying: How We Are Transformed Spiritually as We Die*. 1st ed., HarperSanFrancisco, 1998.

Smith, Rodney. *Lessons from the Dying*. Boston: Wisdom Publications, 1998.

Sontag, Susan. *Illness as Metaphor; and, AIDS and Its Metaphors*. 1st Picador USA ed., Picador USA, 1990.

Spencer-Wendel, Susan, and Witter, Bret. *Until I Say Good-Bye: My Year of Living with Joy*. Harper, 2014.

Stark, Andrew. *The Consolations of Mortality: Making Sense of Death*. Yale University Press, 2016.

Sulmasy, Daniel P. OFM, MD, PhD. A Biopsychosocial-Spiritual Model for the Care of Patients at the End-of-life, *The Gerontologist*, Volume 42, Issue suppl_3, 1 October 2002, Pages 24–33, https://doi-org.ezp-prod1.hul.harvard.edu/10.1093/geront/42.suppl_3.24

Taylor, Jeremy. *Holy Dying: The Rule and Exercises of Holy Dying* in P. G. Stanwood (ed.), *Jeremy Taylor: Holy Living and Holy Dying, Vol. 2: Holy Dying*. Published in print: 1989. Published online: September 2012.

Thaler, Richard H. *Nudge: Improving Decisions about Health, Wealth, and Happiness*. Ed. Cass R. Sunstein. Rev. and expanded ed. ed. New York, N.Y: Penguin, 2009. Print.

Thurston, Angie and Casper ter Kuile, *How We Gather* (Cambridge, MA, 2015).

---, *Something More* (Cambridge, MA, 2016).

Thurston, Angie, Casper ter Kuile, and Sue Phillips, *December Gathering: Notes from the Field* (Cambridge, MA, 2017).

---. *Care of Souls.* (Cambridge, MA, 2018).

Thurston, Angie, Casper ter Kuile, Sue Phillips, Gil Rendle, and Lisa Greenwood, *Faithful* (Cambridge, MA, 2017)

Tisdale, Sallie. *Advice for Future Corpses (and Those Who Love Them): A Practical Perspective on Death and Dying*. Touchstone, 2018.

Toolis, Kevin. *My Father's Wake: How the Irish Teach Us to Live, Love and Die*. Weidenfeld & Nicolson, 2017.

United Nations. "Universal Declaration of Human Rights." http://www.un.org/en/universal-declaration-human-rights/ Accessed 9 Dec 2017.

USA Today. "Biden on grief, and what might have been." 16 Nov 2017. Print.

Warraich, Haider. *Modern Death: How Medicine Changed the End-of-life.* First edition. New York: St. Martin's Press, 2017.

Watt, Helen. *Life and Death in Health Care Ethics: A Short Introduction.* London; New York: Routledge, 2000.

Weiner, Jonathan. *His Brother's Keeper: A Story from the Edge of Medicine.* 1st ed. New York, N.Y.: Ecco, 2004.

Wilder, Thornton. *The Bridge of San Luis Rey.* Boni, 1927. (Kindle edition).

Wright AA, et. al. *JAMA.* "Associations between end-of-life discussions, patient mental health, medical care near death, and caregiver bereavement adjustment." 8 Oct 2008. Online.

Zinsser, William Knowlton. *Writing about Your Life: a Journey into the Past.* Marlowe & Co., 2004.

Zitter, Jessica Nutik. *Extreme Measures: Finding a Better Path to the End-of-life.* New York: Penguin Random House, 2017.

ACKNOWLEDGMENTS

"If the only prayer you ever say in your entire life is thank you, it will be enough." ~Meister Eckhart

My deepest thanks to many generous and helpful supporters. Your belief helped keep hope alive.

Holy Angels friend and Index Card Cure collaborator: Jane Collen

WISP (Writing—Intentional Spiritual Practice): Kris, Mary, and Mary Kay for their support, encouragement and accountability

Namaste sisters: Kris, Aleta, Ginny, Lee, Kathy, Mary Jo, Minhthu, Barb, Anne, Matilde, Kay

Stories from Susan Clark, Kris Casey, Dolphy Fairhurst, Donna Parry, Katherine Powers, Mary Kay Schoen, Kay Sempel, Kathy Silvia.

Encouragement from Susan, Jim, Kris, Susan, Jane, Nell, Cheryle, Clare, Andrea, Anne, Virgie, Anne, Sue, Kathy, Carol, Juli, Arlington book group, Sherry 11 (Tracy, Ann, Lynne, Delna, Marty, Mary, Melissa, Patti, Sharon, EthelMary, Cathi, Katherine, Anne), our siblings, Army Arlington Ladies, and West Point 1980 classmates. Your prayers, messages, meals, and love have been a blessing.

AAFMAA: A. E. Lyne Babin, Steve Galing, Matt Hicks, Erin Jones, Mike Meese, Young Park, Rob Rea

Beta Readers: Collin Agee, Dan Grey, Bill Lynagh for their deep read and comments about the manuscript.

Editors Karen Moseley and Linda Hughes

Contributors to the chapter for young families – Steven and Emily Grey

Alan and Florence Salisbury – who believed in me and *Good Goodbyes* without even seeing the manuscript.

With love and special thanks to Dan, Steven, Emily, Rachel, Allison, and Patrick. You make me smile. Love you forever.

About The Author

Joan Grey graduated from West Point in the first class with women and was commissioned in the Army in May 1980. She served in the US and Germany as a platoon leader, commander, and staff officer until injuries from a parachute accident led to a medical discharge. The accident ended her military career but opened her eyes to hospital chaplaincy. She completed chaplaincy training and served at Wake Medical Center in NC, Tampa General Hospital and Moffitt Cancer Center in FL. During her husband's military service, frequent moves resulted in an eclectic career path including additional employment as an environmental educator, fundraiser, facilitator, and numerous volunteer positions to include time as a hospice volunteer. In addition to an undergraduate degree from West Point, she has graduate degrees from San Jose State and Harvard. *Good Goodbyes: A Mortal's Guide to Life* distills research from her thesis: "Awakening to Mortality: End-of-Life as Rite of Passage and Pathway to Transformation," which fulfilled requirements for a Master's in Religion from Harvard. A September

2021 diagnosis of pancreatic cancer has provided an opportunity to test and validate the premise of *Good Goodbyes* that preparation before expiration makes it possible to live fully and consciously all the way until the end.

Endnotes

1   Revelation 21:5 NIV

2   JSG ∞ Jan 2021

3   Life happens while we're making other plans. Allen Saunders. "Quotable Quotes" Reader's Digest, January 1957. Quote is attributed to Saunders, but the line was made famous as a lyric in the Lennon ballad to his 5-year-old son. "Beautiful Boy," released the year Lennon was murdered at age 40

4   JSG, Jan 2021

5   Brené Brown

6   Unknown author; sometimes attributed to boxer Joe Lewis

7   Pew Research Center 2014 *Religious Landscape Study* http://www.pewresearch.org/fact-tank/2015/11/10/most-americans-believe-in-heaven-and-hell/

8   The idea of afterlife as "home" may not resonate with agnostics and atheists. I admit. I don't know, but I imagine a benign universe, not a blank emptiness.

9   Anna Sewell, *Black Beauty*

10   http://www.theclearingnw.com/blog/spiritual-beings-having-a-human-experience

11   Harvard Religious Literacy Project https://rlp.hds.harvard.edu/our-approach/four-principles

12   Pew Research Center study: http://www.pewforum.org/2018/04/25/when-americans-say-they-believe-in-god-what-do-they-mean/

13   70.6% Christian, 23% unaffiliated, 6% non-Christian

14   Pew Research Center. Religious Landscape Study. http://www.pewforum.org/religious-landscape-study/

15   Albom, Mitch. Tuesdays with Morrie: an Old Man, a Young Man, and Life's Greatest Lesson. 1st ed., Doubleday, 1997. 222.

16   McLeod, S. A. (2018, May 03). Erik Erikson's stages of psychosocial development. Retrieved from https://www.simplypsychology.org/Erik-Erikson.html

17   Moore, PSYC E-1770 lecture on Deci and Ryan's Self-Determination Theory (SDT), Jan 2018.

18   The 1991 Patient Self-Determination Act instituted advance directives (AD) to extend autonomy and safeguard wishes for health care. An AD allows patients to indicate desires for pain control as well as interventions such as cardiopulmonary resuscitation (CPR), breathing tubes, tube feeding, or dialysis.

19   "GULLIVER'S TRAVELS into Several REMOTE NATIONS OF THE WORLD." The Project Gutenberg eBook of Gulliver's Travels, by Jonathan Swift, www.gutenberg.org/files/829/829-h/829-h.htm. Part 3, Chapter 10.

20   John 12:24 NIV - - Bible Gateway

21   Quote attributed to boxer Joe Lewis. The Complete Annotated
     Grateful Dead Lyrics edited by David G. Dodd, Alan Trist.
     353.

22   https://healthcare.findlaw.com/patient-rights/what-is-the-
     uniform-declaration-of-death-act-or-udda.html

23   Marie Curie

24   Kochanek, 1.

25   https://www.cdc.gov/nchs/fastats/life-expectancy.htm

26   Thanks to Lee Hofmann for mentioning the Time Remaining
     number

27   https://www.ssa.gov/planners/lifeexpectancy.html

28   Chart created using statistics extracted from CDC data https://
     webappa.cdc.gov/cgi-bin/broker.exe

29   https://www.cdc.gov/mmwr/volumes/70/wr/mm7014e1.htm

30   Increases in opioid addiction and suicide rates are also
     shortening average life expectancy.

31   Kochanek, "Mortality in the United States, 2016." Harrington,
     71-72.

32   http://www.newyorker.com/magazine/2007/04/30/the-way-
     we-age-now

33   Death Café's objective is 'to increase awareness of death with
     a view to helping people make the most of their (finite) lives'.
     https://deathcafe.com/

34   Harrington, 71.

35   Source: Lunney JR, Lynn J, Foley D, et al; Patterns of
     Functional Decline at the End of Life. JAMA. 2003;289(18):
     2387-2392. https://www.mypcnow.org/copy-of-fast-fact-325

36   Schneider, 98.

37   Schneider, 94.

38   https://www.wsj.com/articles/
SB10001424052970203918304577243321242833962

39   Elisabeth Kubler-Ross

40   Online Etymology Dictionary

41   Online Etymology Dictionary

42   Kleinman, et al., 355.

43   Gawande, New Yorker, 55.

44   Lily Tomlin

45   Mark Twain (1835 – 1910)

46   Thanks to Anne Murphy for this gem.

47   Privacy rules and reporting mean those numbers could be substantially different.

48   Thesis reference / AWARE section

49   To read about the difficulty of choosing appropriate therapies, see physician written books: Being Mortal and When Breath Becomes Air

50   PSAS document

51   https://fivewishes.org/shop/order

52   Six states (Indiana, Kansas, New Hampshire, Ohio, Oregon, Texas) require their own proprietary forms. A resident of those states can use the Five Wishes to identify preferences, but must also complete the state document.

53   may be called proxy, surrogate, agent, representative, or health care power of attorney; different terms that mean the same thing. As if this topic isn't already hard enough, let's also make it confusing?

54   https://www.washingtonpost.com/local/public-safety/i-am-determined-to-have-a-different-ending-to-my-story-woman-

wrote-before-murder/2016/10/25/ddb9ef48-2c74-4e89-a928-5be0c647998a_story.html

55   Attributed to publisher Malcolm Forbes

56   William Morris, 19th century designer

57   Peace Pilgrim

58   You may want to consider a bank safety deposit box for storing difficult-to-replace documents. Just make sure that you let your family know what bank and where the key is located.

59   Attributed to Theodor Geisel, better known as Dr. Seuss, but quote investigators have not found it in his writing.

60   https://www.deathwithdignity.org/learn/religion-spirituality/

61   https://www.thehastingscenter.org/briefingbook/physician-assisted-death/

62   https://khn.org/news/article/montana-medical-aid-in-dying-legal-gray-zone-reviving-legislation/?utm_campaign=KHN%3A%20Daily%20Health%20Policy%20Report&utm_medium=email&_hsmi=118659665&_hsenc=p2ANqtz-9YQY-lBp7c8eV_q8uRLSlodNcngOCoaUomk8R87qwgmRmoDiiXJV7ugzpG6AbPbs9Zxw-tXEZE3pmSD9Dr4i_bSeXLUA&utm_content=118659665&utm_source=hs_email

63   Diane Rehm. When My Time Comes, 165.

64   Tisdale, 135.

65   Dying Well final lecture, slide 14 https://palliative.stanford.edu/home-hospice-home-care-of-the-dying-patient/where-do-americans-die/ Probably close to 100% would prefer to skip dying all together...

66   Gawande, Atul. Being Mortal: Medicine and what Matters in the End. New York: Metropolitan Books/Henry Holt and

Company, 2014. Print. 177.

67   Byock,

68   Rule of St. Benedict: instruction for those embracing a
      monastic lifestyle, Chapter 4 "The Instruments of Good
      Works, 4.47.
      http://www.gutenberg.org/files/50040/50040-h/50040-h.
      html#chapter-4-nl-what-are-the-instruments-of-good-works

69   Steve Jobs' reported last words: https://www.nytimes.
      com/2011/10/30/opinion/mona-simpsons-eulogy-for-steve-
      jobs.html?pagewanted=all

70   Notes from a spiritual retreat at Graymoor, NY in 1991 or '92.

71   Bumper sticker slogan: National Donor Awareness Week is the
      first week of August each year. World Organ Donation Day is
      on August 6th annually.

72   https://www.organdonor.gov/about/facts-terms/donation-
      myths-facts.html

73   Registering is simple. Visit www.life-source.org and click on
      "Register as a Donor."

74   https://www.everplans.com/articles/13-different-religious-
      perspectives-on-cremation

75   Mitch Albom, Tuesdays with Morrie, 137.

76   Your Money or Your Life, 51.

77   Henry David Thoreau

78   Matthew 25:23

79   David Rossi, "Criminal Minds." "The Internet Is Forever,"
      2010

80   Attributed to Albert Einstein

81   TS Eliot, Four Quartets

82   http://trymyrabbi.com/sermons/tim-russert-remembered-

fathers-day

83 Thornton Wilder, The Bridge of San Luis Rey

84 Mitch Albom, Tuesdays with Morrie

85 Mary Oliver, "When Death Comes"

86 Gawande, 238.

87 C.S. Lewis

88 Psalm 90:10 NIV - Bible Gateway, 2021, www.biblegateway.com/passage/?search=Psalm%2B90%3A10&version=NIV.

89 The bonus years after 65 herald a passage into elderhood with release from the tyranny of schedules and having time, health, and money. Post-65 lottery: eligible for a federal Social Security pension, and qualify for health care under Medicare. Longevity, health care, and income comprise a trifecta of opportunity. Few routinely celebrate winning this genetic and social lottery.

90 Dr. Seuss

91 Do you favor quality or quantity of life, vitality or vital signs Do you believe pain and suffering are penitential and necessary for attaining the afterlife?

92 http://www.pewforum.org/2013/11/21/religious-groups-views-on-end-of-life-issues/
    https://www.deathwithdignity.org/learn/religion-spirituality/

93 I acknowledge the help of my classmate, Collin Agee.

94 United States Military Academy Alma Mater

95 Key terms compilation based on chaplaincy experiences and consulting these sources:
    https://www.gmc-uk.org/guidance/ethical_guidance/end_of_life_glossary_of_terms.asp
    https://theconversationproject.org/wp-content/uploads/2015/06/Glossary-of-Terms.pdf

https://www.ncbi.nlm.nih.gov/pmc/articles/PMC2772257/

https://www.americanbar.org/content/dam/aba/publications/
probate_property_magazine/v15/05/2001_aba_rpte_pp_
v15_5_article_williams_end_of_life_care_organ_donation_
decisions.authcheckdam.pdf

https://www.americanbar.org/content/dam/aba/administrative/
law_aging/2014_default_surrogate_consent_statutes.
authcheckdam.pdf

https://organdonor.gov/about.html

https://www.americanbar.org/groups/public_education/
resources/law_issues_for_consumers/patient_self_
determination_act.html

http://polst.org/about/polst-and-advance-directives/

96   https://www.hhs.gov/hipaa/for-professionals/security/laws-
regulations/index.html

97   https://oktodie.com/pdf/PSAS.Form.Final.pdf